The Rose of Five Petals

The Rose Of Five Petals

A Path for the Christian Mystic

BETSY SERAFIN

A CROSSROAD BOOK
The Crossroad Publishing Company
New York

1997
The Crossroad Publishing Company
370 Lexington Avenue, New York, NY 10017

Printed in the United States of America

Scripture texts in this work, unless otherwise indicated,
are taken from the New Revised Standard Version of the Bible,
copyright 1989 by the Division of Christian Education of the
National Council of the Churches of Christ in the USA.

Library of Congress Cataloging-in-Publication Data

Serafin, Betsy.
  The rose of five petals : a path for the Christian
mystic / Betsy Serafin.
        p.   cm.
  Includes bibliographical references.
  ISBN 0-8245-1650-8 (pbk.)
      1. Mysticism. 2. Spiritual life—Christianity.
  I. Title.
  BV5082.2.S47   1997
  248.2'2—dc21   97-3915
                                                       CIP

WITH LOVE I DEDICATE THIS *ROSE*
TO MY HUSBAND BOB
AND TO OUR CHILDREN,
KATHERINE, JENIFER, JOSEPH, AND ELIZABETH,
FOR WHOM THIS BOOK WAS WRITTEN

Acknowledgments

Many thanks to those critical readers who have encouraged and taught me: my sister Martha MacLeod, Gene Peters, Jane Carlson, Brian Mahan, Carolyn Stollman, Dr. Desmond Cartwright, and Father George Fitzgerald. To my mentors, Trudy Barlow, John Jebsen, Abbot Andrew Miles, Chaplain Will Reller, and those who have made their transition into the heavenly realms, John Eichleman, Nancy Hanson, and Dr. Leonard Kalal. With deep gratitude to Jhershierra Jelsma who inspired and encouraged me to finish the book. In appreciation of Dwal Khul and his insights into Jesus Christ as the Path. To Dr. Susan Anthes and Dr. Edward Miller for their help with my research. And finally, I thank those saints whose lives have been my inspiration.

AND THERE ARE FIVE STRONG PETALS ON WHICH
THE ROSE IS SET AND THEY WERE CALLED
SALVATIONS AND NOW THEY ARE KNOWN AS
FIVE GATES. AND THIS ROSE IS CALLED THE CUP
OF BLESSING, OF WHICH IT IS SAID: "I WILL TAKE
UP THE CUP OF SALVATION. . . . " [Ps. 116:13]

— *Zohar*

I AM THE ROSE OF SHARON. . . .
— *Song of Solomon 2:1 (KJV)*

Contents

I WALK BEFORE THE LORD
IN THE LAND OF THE LIVING.
—*Psalm 116:9*

Preface

*T*his book is about the mystical Path, a path that leads us back into our divine heritage: union with God. At first I thought that one should have entered into that union before presuming to write about such things. I realize now, however, that if divine union were complete, the need to write about getting there might not exist. Once that heavenly state is reached, the desires to proselytize, to convert, and to save, hold little attraction. Jesus never wrote a word, and he never tried to convince anyone of anything; he simply was (is) the Path. So I am writing while I am still struggling with myself and have an urge to expound on how I understand the path that Jesus laid before us. None of this would have been possible for me, however, without the years I spent studying the major religions of the world, which have given me a fuller understanding of Christianity and its concealed messages.

Because of its uniqueness, the life of Jesus Christ will be the template for this book. The life of Jesus was filled with symbols, words, and actions designed to be a parable for all who strive toward union with God. Jesus spoke, not as a man, but as Christ. His life was a paradigm of perfection for each of us to follow. But if we point to Jesus and say, "Look what he could do," we have missed the message, for he came to show us not what he could do, but what we can do. We have the choice to accept the promises of scripture, or to continue to walk in limitation.

Jesus, in his birth, baptism, transfiguration, crucifixion, and resurrection, revealed the "five gates of salvation" that we find in the *Zohar*.[1] The ancients comprehended these gates as the five initiations. In the Christian system these gates, or initiations are:

1. Birth in a cave
2. Baptism by water
3. Baptism by fire (transfiguration)
4. Crucifixion
5. Resurrection/Ascension

In the ancient system these same initiations were called:

1. Cave Initiation
2. Stream Initiation
3. Initiation of Tents or Ascent of the Holy Mountain
4. Night Sea Journey
5. Born Again or Resurrection

This ancient system is represented, mystically, as the five base petals of a rose. The ancient heroes in mythology underwent these same five initiations that were then brought to fruition in the life of Jesus. Each of us is challenged by these same initiations. When Jesus invited us to take up the cross and follow in his footsteps, he called us to tread (symbolically) the path he had taken to come into union with his own divine nature. Jesus Christ was man/God. Had he been solely divine from his birth, there would be no hope for us. He came to show us the way—he became the Way. Now it is for us to tread the Way of the Cross, to die to our lower nature that we might rise with Christ in the age to come—the reign of heaven.

The Rose of Five Petals will take each of us step by step through the same initiations that were experienced in the life of Jesus. His story is our story. Christ, the Higher Self within each of us, will be our guide along the Path. This One, within, will lead us as we:

Put our lives in order
Transform our emotions
Take on the mind of Christ
Walk the Way of the Cross
Become Beings of Light

In *The Hymn of the Universe,* Teilhard de Chardin, the French Jesuit, wrote what has been called a dangerous prayer. I have prayed this prayer almost daily for some twenty years. As we begin the Path, I invite you who dare, you who are ready to become who we were created to be (Christed Beings), to pray this transforming prayer with me—each day:

O Lord, lock me up
Enfold me in the deepest
Depths of thine heart
And then holding me there
Refine me
Purify me
Kindle me
Set me ablaze
And lift me aloft
till I become utterly what
Thou wouldst have me become
Through the cleansing death
Of self.
Amen[2]

Reader's Guide

$\mathcal{B}$efore we delve into the mystery, I am going to digress long enough to clarify a few idiosyncrasies to be found in this text. You will notice that sometimes words are capitalized and at other times the same words are not. Here are some of the terms and how they are intended throughout these pages.

ego = self = soul = psyche = personality
Ego = Christ = Self = Soul = Psyche = Mind = Spirit

The top line represents the undeveloped soul (personality), while the bottom line reflects the evolved Soul, which is that enduring part of us that is impregnated with the light and life of Christ until it becomes pure Spirit.

The more influence Christ has been allowed to have in our lives, the more purified our soul will be. Love and light will fill us as we learn to get out of the way.

Purification is a process that is rarely completed by the end of a lifetime. Jesus tells us that there are many mansions in his Father's house. Earth may be one of the mansions. I see these mansions as temporary dwellings where we will continue to move into the fullness of the Kingdom, and then into the presence of God where the soul will become Soul or Christed Being.

My Story

$\mathcal{L}$et us imagine a series of books that were written to hold all the secrets of the universe. Each of these books was written in a different language, a different style, and in each book the main character was given a new name. And even before the books were written, there were legends that told the stories. But beyond this, the writings were uniquely about each of us. You and I are the protagonist in every story. We are the heroes of the myths, the heroines of the fairy tales.

As a child, I read many stories. Among them was a story about a baby boy who was born in a manger that was just inside a cave. He grew up to preach and perform miracles; he was crucified, died, and was resurrected. At that time I did not find the story to be very different from the one about the princess who was locked in a tower and awakened years later by the kiss of a handsome prince. In fact, it was easier for me to identify with the princess and her "resurrection" than it was to see myself as the babe in Bethlehem. No one ever suggested to me that the story of the life of Jesus Christ was my story—your story.

Though our stories have different twists and turns, all have gotten us to where we are today. We are our stories. Each story has its own lessons and its own initiations, because life is a path back to God.

My early childhood in a small town in Kentucky was restrictive, but secure. Life centered around the church. There was no drinking in my home and we didn't go to movies on Sunday. Sunday morning was taken up with Sunday school, church services, and then we often returned in the evening for a potluck supper and another service. Sometimes we went back for Wednesday night services. That routine was typical among the Protestants where we lived. I complied with, and even enjoyed that way of life until I was old enough to want to spend more time with my school friends. Mother's wisdom then allowed me to stretch beyond those early confines. There had been enough family tragedy to make her want me to be happy, and I was.

Mother's wisdom, however, did not extend to Catholicism. When I was between eight and eleven years old, she and I lived two blocks from a large Catholic cathedral, St. Stephen's. I was strictly forbidden to go anywhere near the cathedral—an admonition that was better than a handwritten invitation. I remember walking the opposite direction from that imposing structure and around the block to get there unnoticed. From the time we moved to that part of town, I played a game I called "Church."

The game began by sneaking a lace handkerchief from Mother's small top dresser drawer. I would then tuck the hand-kerchief into my pocket. When I reached the church by my circuitous route, I would look both ways for any of her gossipy friends, take out the handkerchief, and place it carefully on my head. After tiptoeing into that echoing edifice with its grand high ceiling, stone floor, stained-glass windows, and faint smell of incense, I would manage to genuflect (which knee didn't matter). Then, as I knelt on the cushioned kneeler, I pretended to pray while I cautiously observed the few people around me whom I believed to be really praying. The best part, however, was the statues. I watched old women kiss their feet, whereupon I would touch my own lips to that cold stone, which always gave me a shudder. The statues' unflinching faces scared me just enough to make the game exciting, while their smiles suggested they knew my deception. I loved them. When I was alone, I would take a long taper and indiscriminately light candles. Even though I didn't understand the meaning behind any of the ritual, I left with a great sense of inner peace. St. Stephen's was a holy space for me.

It was in my own church, though, that I first came to know that inner reality—Christ. This experience occurred when I was about thirteen. At that time, I still thought Christ was someone apart from me. I didn't understand that Christ was my essence, the core of my being. But in spite of my undeveloped theology, the event changed my life.

We had moved to a more residential neighborhood when I decided to attend our summer church camp. The reason for my decision was less than spiritual; it was because the preacher's son would be there. It was clear that he didn't know I existed, even though our backyards touched corners. Mother could always persuade me to hang out the clothes or bring in some ripe garden tomatoes as I anticipated a glimpse of Allen. But since all my efforts had been in vain, camp was looking better and better as I thought about a week filled with romantic opportunity.

Camp, however, did not open Allen's eyes to what he had been missing just across the back fence. And as the week dragged on, my interest in him waned and my mind turned to the activities of the camp. Then came Friday night, the last night before we would return home.

The stars were shining brightly that night in Kentucky. On top of a mountain, a bonfire was lit at the foot of a huge wooden cross. Singing "Jacobs Ladder," young campers climbed slowly toward the top of the mountain. Something began to stir deep within as we sang the words, "Sinner, do you love my Jesus?" and then, "If you love him, why not serve him?" Tears streamed down my face, and I was unaware of anything going on around me until we had descended the slope and were back in our cabins. The rest of the campers got into their beds as the lights were turned off. But I went quietly outside and followed a path that led deep into the woods, something I would never have dreamed of doing any other time. But on that night, I felt no fear. I was filled with a sense of well-being that I had not known before. Among the trees I fell to my knees and began to pray. There seemed to be a glow of light all around me, and I could see as if it were day. I was filled with incredible joy, knowing that life held nothing to fear. I prayed, but for the greater part of the night it was as if I were in some kind of a trance, breathing in and out the presence of God, reluctant to leave.

On that mountain I had given my life to Christ, though not a word had been spoken. Only years later did I understand what happened that night. Now I realize that the divine spark had been awakened within—the Christ, the I AM. I gave God my free will, though I would spend the rest of my life trying to take it back and then give it again.

The impact of that experience lasted three years. During that time I continued to feel God's presence. I read the Bible with fervor, taught a Sunday school class of small children and in the second year joined a Christian youth group in the high school. In the beginning, I was ever aware of a presence. It was not until my junior year that the experience began to diminish. Then in college it almost disappeared. Christianity was replaced with ideas that I gleaned from the philosophers and writers of history and literature. Today many of those same writings enhance my faith, but at that time there was no one to guide my confused thinking. A sadness entered my soul and I forgot what I had lost. Searching, I went to Europe, where I studied French and political science for a year.

In Geneva, when we weren't in university classes or skiing, we sat in small, smoky coffee houses discussing the merits and demerits of religions and governments. Those were the beginning years of disillusionment with the existing structures. Several years passed. Then in my twenty-fourth year, I met the man I was to marry and he introduced me to Catholicism. I was thrilled to learn the meaning behind my childhood game of "Church" and to recapture some of the inspiration from my mountaintop experience.

Strangely, I found that those years that I thought had been lost were not lost at all. For all of life is part of the Path, just as every experience is for our growth.

OUR JOURNEY CAN BEGIN at any time. It might begin with a deliberate decision to find God. Just as the Buddha said he would sit under the bodhi tree until enlightenment came to him, we too can decide to pursue that elusive One. Or if we have been seeking (though it may not have been in an orthodox fashion), the journey can begin most unexpectedly with a religious experience, as it did for Paul when he was blinded by Christ's light on the road to Damascus.

We take a conscious step toward God when we say "yes" to the invitation to follow Christ. Unfortunately, though, this acceptance of Christ often leads to a narrow view of God as we tend to associate God with the group that extended the invitation. But as time passes and with luck or grace, we may find God beyond the constraints of dogma. Our vision and our understanding will then take on greater and greater dimension, ever more demanding and ever more exciting as we undergo one initiation after another.

AN INITIATION IS usually a formal admission into a secret club or organization. But in the case of the five initiations that were taken by Jesus (the same ones that we must undergo to return to union with God), each initiation is not very formal and not at all so obvious. No one will ring bells or burn incense; but bit by bit we will discover a change of attitude. The things that would have distressed us at one time are seen from a wider perspective. Even tragedy can take on purpose and meaning. *All* is part of who we are becoming.

Gradually our past is seen, not so much as being filled with error (sometimes called sin), as with occasions for growth and understanding. We will recognize that we are who we are today because of who we were yesterday. Without our past suffering and transgressions, we would not have the compassion and humility that we have come to possess. *We may even find that the home and the workplace are more rigorous sites for growth than the cave or the monastery.*

Background/ Theology

JUST AS THE BOUNDARIES OF EARTH'S NATIONS
ARE INVISIBLE TO THE ASTRONAUT VIEWING
OUR PLANET FROM SPACE, SO TOO DO THE
MYSTIC'S EYES REGISTER NO REAL ABSOLUTE
BOUNDARIES BETWEEN RELIGIONS.[1]
—*Ron Miller*

THE MYSTERY

O Dark Mystery
So bright I cannot see
Sometimes hushed
Sometimes clanging in my soul

I enter as You reveal
Darting from tree to tree
Hide and seek
The Mystery

1

Mysticism

For many, mysticism is a scary word that is often associated with fortune tellers and magic. However, in the unabridged *Random House Dictionary* we read that mysticism pertains to "the mysteries (that are) known only to the initiated." In scripture, mystery relates to esoteric or hidden teachings such as those discussed in Matthew 13:10:

> Then the disciples came and asked him, "Why do you speak to them in parables?" He answered, "To you it has been given to know the secrets of the kingdom of heaven, but to them it has not been given."

In John 20:22 Jesus appeared to his disciples and breathed on them (initiated them) with his breath of Life and said, "Receive the Holy Spirit." He promised a Spirit of truth that would lead them safely into the divine mystery (John 16:12-13):

> I still have more things to say to you, but you cannot bear them now. When the Spirit of truth comes, he will guide you into all the truth.

Over the centuries, through the guidance of Spirit, many have received insights which they have passed on to us. We find, for the greater part, that these Souls (saints) have nearly always shared a common experience of oneness and love.

TODAY, THE SPIRIT of God is being poured out upon the world. Old models are collapsing, while new ones are being built. Evil is rampant, while love is greater than ever. Where hatred still persists, many are coming forth to protect the oppressed. It is an exciting, yet demanding, time to be alive.

Just as political systems are in flux, religious traditions are evolving. Since the awakening that followed the Second Vatican Council in the Catholic Church, many priests, monks, and nuns have left the churches, monasteries, and convents with the realization that sanctity, though supported by these communities, can also be found outside of them. Because of this exodus, monastery and convent doors have opened to the laity, making contemplative prayer available to all of us. Today, meditative prayer (the heart of the mystical life) is being taught all over the world so that you and I can enjoy the silence where mysteries are revealed.[1]

Many years ago I heard Father William McNamara, a Carmelite monk, tell about a meeting he had with Rabbi Abraham Heschel on the streets of New York City. This meeting occurred in the early 1960's when few had heard of the upcoming Second Vatican Council in Rome. Father McNamara shared the news of the anticipated conclave with the rabbi, and they began to discuss the probable success or failure of the council. At that point Rabbi Heschel inquired, "How many contemplatives will be attending?" He was asking if the members would be talking, or listening to God. In his mind, the answer would determine the outcome of the council. Father McNamara appreciated the rabbi's wisdom.

Each of us can ask the same question: "Am I talking, or am I listening to God?" The mysteries can be revealed to us only if we choose a disciplined life that hears God from moment to moment.

We will hear the voice of God as we peel away the dense layers of unconsciousness that surround and suffocate us. This peeling is the suffering of the cross, sacrifice; for each layer that is peeled away represents a death. This dying creates a path of renunciation and purification for those who are ready.

The late Trappist monk Thomas Merton wrote:

> Without trying to make of the Christian life a cult of suffering for its own sake, we must frankly admit that self-denial and sacrifice are absolutely essential to the life of prayer.[2]

This sacrifice, however, is only a release of the lesser for the greater. We are called to bring order into our lives, and that requires sacrifice. Happily, we are asked to relinquish only those things that make us miserable: worldly attachments and mundane desires. It is the attachment to things we may lose and a desire for things we may never have that bring about fear and suffering.

Introspection sheds light into our darkness and reveals our attachments, desires, and fears. Gradually we recognize that all must be given to Christ to be transformed. Finally, we are aware that creation belongs wholly to God. Nothing is ours; we are but stewards. With this realization comes freedom.

Freedom begins with a taste of the divine. Few of us have not had some experience outside our ability to comprehend, an experience beyond the senses, a mystical experience. We recognize such an event as a time of grace, a gift from God. Having had an encounter with the holy, we know that there is something more than what we see around us. At that sacred moment, a desire is kindled within us to enter God's Kingdom.

In the Christian religion, the Kingdom of Heaven is found in God or Christ, the hidden mystery. Mystery sees all, knows all, and is all. Mystery is not an object to be grasped but the common denominator in all of creation lying just beyond reason and the senses. Mystery can be revealed to us at any moment through no effort at all. Or in meditation, it may come in the deepest silence. In other religions and philosophies, the mystery is called Atman, Nirvana, Tien, Tao, Torah, and Wisdom. Mystery lies beyond, behind, and even within nature. God/Christ, the heart of all mystery, is nearer than we are to ourselves.

The experience of the mystic is that, while God transcends nature, the divine is simultaneously to be found in all of creation and cannot be separated from it. In the first chapter of Ephesians Paul reveals that God

> And he has put all things under his feet and has made him the head over all things for the church, which is his body, the fullness of him who fills all in all.

Thus we can conclude that all of creation is intrinsically divine.

THE PATH OF THE MYSTIC is the way of the cross. For the Christian, this path follows the life of Jesus Christ, and that is what this book is about. It is the incarnation of the Christ in the life of Jesus that brings us hope of a return to our sacred heritage. Theologians tell us that Jesus Christ was one hundred percent human and one hundred percent divine, which is called hypostatic union. Jesus and Christ became one as he followed the Path, showing us the way—becoming the Way. Once union was achieved, he earned the title Jesus the Christ or Jesus Christ. As revealed by the star, Jesus was the one who was preordained to take us to the next level of consciousness in our spiritual evolution. Jesus, our elder brother, became our Lord and Savior.

If Jesus had not been human, he could not have died. But just as Jesus was human and divine, you and I are human and divine. With the crucifixion, Jesus died to his human nature and took on his full divinity as he was resurrected. He expected us to do the same when he said:

> If any want to become my followers, let them deny themselves and take up their cross and follow me.[3]

Then he declared that we would do even greater works than he did[4] . . . and we will because Christ lives in us. The life of Jesus created a path for us to follow. The variations on the Path will be as many as there are people, but there are guidelines that will help us no matter what our diversities might be. The Path leads Home.

THE PATH

With pain and joy you etched the Path
and called us each to follow.
Most have said, "That's very nice" and
thanked you for your sacrifice.

Still you hold the cross up high inviting
each of us to "die."
We bow with deep serenity, but decline
to hang upon your tree.

2

𝒯ℎℯ 𝒫𝒶𝓉ℎ

𝓜any have come to show us the way, but none has become the Way except Jesus the Christ. In his birth, life, death, and resurrection, Jesus portrayed the ultimate path to God.

In studying the Path, we will discover ourselves. We will walk through the numerous aspects of each level beginning with the Cave Initiation (the Level of Order, the physical realm). It is on this level that we will allow the light of Christ to shine into our darkness, bringing order into our lives.

Then in the Stream Initiation (the Level of Will, the emotional or feeling realm), we will begin the death to our own selfish egos by inviting Christ to heal our emotions. This Level of Will is perhaps the most difficult of the five levels.

Next, we move to the Initiation of Tents or Tabernacles (the Level of Wisdom, the mental realm) where we will experience the presence of God in all we do as our minds are transformed, just as Jesus was transformed on the Mount of the Transfiguration.

But there is still the Night Sea Journey (the Level of Justice that will complete the three levels that have preceded it). This fourth level demands the crucifixion of our lower nature, death to the selfish ego. This death anticipates our rise with Christ in the fifth initiation of Love that is fulfilled in the resurrection and ascension of Jesus.

| | | THE PATH | |
| | | A Model for Reference | |

LEVEL	ELEMENT	NAMES OF THE INITIATIONS	
		(ANCIENT)	(CHRISTIAN)
ORDER Physical	EARTH	CAVE INITIATION	BIRTH/INCARNATION
WILL Emotional Feeling	WATER	STREAM INITIATION or SECRET OF THE SEA	BAPTISM OF WATER
WISDOM Mental	FIRE	INITIATION OF TENTS OR TABERNACLE or ASCENT OF THE HOLY MOUNTAIN	CONFIRMATION BAPTISM OF FIRE (Transfiguration)
JUSTICE Physical Emotional Mental	EARTH WATER FIRE	NIGHT SEA JOURNEY	CRUCIFIXION
LOVE Spiritual	AIR	BORN AGAIN / RESURRECTION	RESURRECTION / ASCENSION
		All Levels Are Within ••• The Only Way Out Is In	

The model above will be helpful throughout our journey.

Each of us is aware of something deep within, something with which we long to be united, something we cannot grasp. We recognize this *something* as the very essence of our being, but we are unable to identify it. Something (someone) is calling us Home. We lean forward to listen, but it speaks too softly in the midst of our noise. We sense that it is our primordial Mother, our Father. We yearn to know our Creator, our Lord, but the world lures us to its shores like the sirens who sang to Odysseus. Only those truly dedicated souls who have gone before us have managed to find their way past the rocks of destruction and have reached their destination. Now it is for us to find our way.

HOW WELL I REMEMBER my first determination to begin the Path, to find my way. That urgency began about a year after we moved to Boulder, Colorado around 1974. I had learned to meditate through Transcendental Meditation because that was the only method readily available at the time, and I found it to be a good teaching. In those days, Christianity didn't offer this practice to the laity. Being anxious for a really deep prayer experience, I decided to attend a two-week-long meditation with a group of Buddhists that was given on Gold Hill in the mountains near Boulder.

When I arrived at the site, I discovered that we were expected to rise at 4:30 A.M. and meditate until 9:30 P.M. Our diet was a strict issue of fruits, vegetables, and grains. We were not allowed eye contact, nor were we to speak, read, or write. I am sure if I were to meet my roommate from that retreat today, we would be total strangers.

In the middle of the first week, an abnormally early snow storm moved into the camp, making the cabins (most having lost their mortar) freezing cold. As the wind blew through the chinks between the logs, we sat from morning till night buried in our sleeping bags. The sleeping bag did, however, have the advantage of hiding my less than erect meditation posture.

On the eighth day the sun came out again; but it was too late for me. Thinking I might expire at any moment, I signed up for a ten-minute visit with the retreat master. When my turn came, I bowed from the waist, and then began to complain of my intense discomfort; I had decided that my back was gradually disintegrating. I assured the director that if I didn't go home that day, an ambulance would have to carry me down the mountain. Whereupon he inquired, "You are a Christian?" I could not imagine how he knew, but I replied that I was. Then he said, rather matter-of-factly, "My wife is a Christian." That was a surprise. Finally he addressed my pain: "Did your Lord not hang upon the cross, and did he not suffer there?" Shaken, I had no reply. He continued, "Can you not hang there with him a bit longer?" I was touched that a Buddhist could speak with such understanding on the deepest level of my faith. Humbled, I returned to my cushion.

This time, instead of starting right in with meditation, I prayed, "Lord, may my discomfort be redemptive. May it contribute in some small way to the plan of salvation." And then I began to meditate. After about forty minutes, I had a most unusual experience. There was a silent pop, and I could no longer feel my body. I could see my body, but the pain was gone. Just at that moment, an ant crossed the floor in front of me. I have never loved anything more than I loved that ant. Tears of joy came to my eyes as I realized that I was thinking with the mind of God who had created the ant and me. I realized how much I must be loved, how much God must love every one of us.

If only I could have sustained the experience. But progress was made during that week. The layers of self-hatred had begun to peel away. I received what I had come for, the touch of the Blessed One.

Meditation allows the unconscious mind to release the burdens that life has put upon us. This process can take years, but an intensive time like the days I spent on Gold Hill can move one along the Path with giant steps, though it is not without pain.

I remember a young girl sitting directly in front of me on the floor who would sob from time to time. I wanted so badly to reach out and give her some comfort, but I had been advised that even eye contact would interfere with the inner work. I understood, in retrospect, what I would have lost if someone had reached out to me in the midst of my pain. There are times to minister to one another, and there are times when we only impede the work of Spirit—the true Comforter.

MYTHS OF THE ANCIENT heroines and heroes are all stories of pain and success, allegories of the struggle along the Path. These fables foreshadow the birth, life, death, and resurrection of Jesus Christ. In the fifth century St. Augustine wrote:

> . . . that which is called the Christian religion existed among the ancients, and never did not exist from the beginning of the human race until Christ came in the flesh, at which time the true religion, which already existed, began to be called Christianity.[1]

Long before the birth of Jesus, there were heroes and heroines who followed the Path. There were mystery schools built on myths depicting the life of one born in a cave of a virgin. This hero was called light-bringer, healer, savior, mediator, or deliverer. The hero led a life of turmoil for humankind, was vanquished by the powers of darkness, often descended into hell, and rose again. These stories surrounded the lives of Hercules, Krishna, Attis, Osiris, Horus, Dionysus, Mithras, Quetzalcoatl, Tammuz, Adonis, and many others. Upon these stories, churches were built into which disciples were received by baptism and the god was commemorated with a eucharistic meal. There has been much written on the heroes and heroines who were known as sun gods or gods and goddesses of vegetation and resurrection.

The hero, a paradigm of virtue, was one who received a call from above. This one knew that a higher force was drawing him or her toward an almost insurmountable task. The road to be followed held many obstacles, such as dragons, mountains, wide bodies of water to cross, giants, and evil spirits. The impediments would be overcome, even though the courageous life of the hero/heroine would often be lost—most often to rise again.

The hero, who was warrior, lover, servant, and king was usually born of a human, but conceived of a god. Many of these heroes probably began as actual historical persons whose stories became embellished over the years. An example of one of these mythical heroes was Krishna (Christ in Greek) who was considered to be an incarnation of Vishnu, the second person of the Hindu trinity, the one who incarnates: the Son.

Lord Krishna was believed to have lived about three thousand years before Christ and was said to have been born of a virgin in a cave. Like Christ, his birth was announced by a star. His enemies tried to destroy him with a massacre of infant boys. He was to have performed many miracles, and it is even told that he raised the dead. Arjuna was his beloved disciple before whom he was transfigured. His death is related in different ways. One version says that he was shot by an arrow, while another says he was crucified on a tree. Then he descended into hell and rose again from the dead. He ascended into heaven in the sight of many people, while he is expected to return to be judge of the living and the dead.[2] In the *Bhagavad Gita*, Krishna declares, "I am the oblation, I am the sacrifice, I am the ancestral offering."

Since the life of Jesus was so uncanny in its similarities to those of the mystery heroes, it is not surprising that Christianity appeared to the Greeks and Romans as another mystery religion from the East. It was for this reason that the early church sought to denigrate and even to destroy the myths. The church fathers and later clergy complained that the devil had used the Christian rites of baptism, breaking of bread, and images of death and resurrection to confuse Christian believers. An example of this narrow-mindedness is found in the Yucatan, where Christian missionaries accused the devil of planting the story of Quetzalcoatl (a hero with a story similar to that of Jesus) in the minds of the Indians. But in spite of the church's attempt to disassociate itself from the myths and the cults that surrounded them, Christianity held strong similarities, both liturgically and ideologically, to early cultic worship. In the mystery cults, whether by the sacramental eating of a corn cake or the flesh of a sacrificed animal, the eating of the body and drinking the blood was considered participation in the life of the god. Cosmically, the stage had been set for the birth of Jesus in a cave on the outskirts of Bethlehem.

The early church, however, was not ready to accept this connection between cultic rites and those instituted by Jesus Christ. The church fathers built their liturgy on the words of the Last Supper without acknowledging its archetypal roots. Because of this refusal to make the connection between the old and the new, an opportunity for understanding was lost as it is today when we look at the differences and cannot see the similarities between religions and denominations.

I ONLY BEGAN TO comprehend Christianity as I studied Hinduism and meditated with the Buddhists. If we could become more knowledgeable about other religions and their historical influence on Christianity, our prejudices would dissolve one by one. Dr. Raimundo Panikkar, a Harvard professor, has suggested that as our understanding expands, we realize that Christianity is but a link, though a critical one, in the history of God's revelation:

> The Church is centered upon the authentic and living person of Jesus Christ . . . in actual fact the claim of the Church is not that she is the religion for the whole of mankind but that she is the place where Christ is fully revealed, the end and plenitude of every religion.[3]

Because of the revelation of Christ in Jesus, I now understand my own ultimate reality, for it is the Christ in me that longs to reveal itself. What an incredible relief it has been to know that the core of my being is absolute goodness. The feeling is akin to waking from a bad dream. We don't hold guilt or anger from a dream; why then should negative and worrisome thoughts persist from a life experience? After a difficult incident, a stupid reaction, hurting another, or being hurt, I can say with conviction, "Thank God that is not who I am," for my essence is divine. I am forgiven, I forgive and take personal responsibility for my actions, while I amend my ways knowing that all that went before is used for my growth and understanding. Dwelling on the incident only perpetuates the nightmare. Each day is a new awakening in the Kingdom; for the Hero/Christ is my true identity. I AM.

Christ is the hero who dwells within each of us, the warrior who will slay the serpent (carnal knowledge, sin, separation) and lead us to salvation. Not only must we recognize the divine warrior, but we must participate in the divine life by eating the body and drinking the blood of the sacrificed animal, which can be understood as consuming and being consumed by the divine.

It is God who has given us the many archetypes of this hero, and it is God who sent the first-born Son as revelation of the archetypes that had gone before in mythology.

TO SUMMARIZE: In the ancient system, the first initiation was called the Cave Initiation and was exemplified by the birth and burial of Jesus in a cave. The second, the Stream Initiation, can be seen in the baptism of Jesus by John the Baptist. The third was known as the Initiation of Tents (booths) or Tabernacles such as those suggested by Peter, James, and John at the scene of Jesus' transfiguration on the mountain when the disciples said:

> Lord, it is good for us to be here; if you wish, I will make three dwellings here, one for you, one for Moses, and one for Elijah.
>
> —Matthew 17:4

The fourth initiation, the Night Sea Journey or Crucifixion, calls to mind the passage in Matthew where Jesus foretold the following:

> For just as Jonah was three days and three nights in the belly of the sea monster, so for three days and three nights the Son of Man will be in the heart of the earth.
>
> —Matthew 12:40

The fifth and last initiation (within the realm of physical existence) was called Resurrection, re-birth, or being born again. This initiation was reflected in the resurrection and ascension of the master Jesus, which portrays the final stage of union with God. These stages will be for us the Path (see chart page 31).

Jesus' life was the historical fulfillment of an archetypal pattern for enlightenment. When he commissioned his disciples to follow in his footsteps,[4] he was not merely showing us what he could do, but was demonstrating in a very concrete way what each of us must do. He gave us the ultimate path, a path to be emulated. As we allow our lives to be brought into order, relinquish our will, take on the mind of Christ,[5] and die to the false ego, we will then rise with Christ to new life.

Like particles of light we will return to our Source,
maintaining our myriad of rainbow colors, yet one
with the great Sun.

But before we can climb upon this Path, before we can even accept that there is a path, we must ask, "Why do we need a path? . . . Why the suffering and pain? . . . Why did God give us free will? . . . Why were we allowed to tumble out of our love relationship with the Holy One? . . . Why the Fall?"

LUCIFER

From heaven he fell
Full of light
Cooling in the atmosphere
Of earth
Light became dark
Life became death
Like lava as it reaches
The sea
Vibrant movement hardened
Into stagnant rock

And here we stand
Immortalized in this rock
Immovable impressions

3

The Fall

$\mathcal{B}$efore there was sun, moon, or stars, God began creation with an outburst of Being, declaring, "Let there be light," and there was light. Then the light was separated from the darkness, setting the scene for what was to come. In omniscience, God knew and awaited the Fall, humanity's apparent separation from God.

The theologian Paul Tillich called it "the fall upward," while St. Augustine exclaimed, "Oh happy Fall!" The Fall was part of God's great plan for our growth. Just as our children mature through experience, all of us learn and grow from our positive and negative encounters with life.

Humanity moved away from God and said, "I'd rather do it myself." This desire for independence has created the lessons that come with separation from God. We see that the question is not, "Was there a Fall?" but "What was the Fall and how does it affect you and me?"

THERE IS A STORY that is told about a lioness who was about to attack a flock of sheep when she gave birth to a cub and then died. The baby lion grew up with the sheep and would bleat and eat grass all day long. Then one day another lion happened along and observed this strange behavior. Immediately he took it upon himself to teach this feline how to be a lion. He taught the lion to roar and to do all the things that a proper lion should do.

It is much the same since the Fall. We no longer remember who we are. We have forgotten that we can enjoy a divine relationship with God. We have forgotten we are Spirit and that we can walk on water. We have joined forces with the world and learned how mediocre the life of the flesh can be. We live in loneliness, deception, and illusion. From the time of the Fall until the coming of Jesus, the Lion of Judah,[1] we have immersed ourselves in darkness and in what appears to be separation from God and from one another.

Knowing that in God's reality there can be no separation, many theologians today have denied the Fall. And, of course, they are right. However, the fact that we think we are separate from God is in itself a fallen condition: illusion.

Though we look to the allegory of Eve and the serpent to explain the Fall, the idea of separation from God was portrayed long before the garden scene. Separation, which began with the story of Lucifer's fall from heaven, fulfilled the ancient axiom, "As above, so below."[2]

It could be said that Lucifer was the first to use, or to abuse, free will. This angel was called the Light-Bearer because, prior to the celestial rebellion, there was only Light, Spirit. In this story, we are shown how the angel fell to earth to reign as prince of the world.[3] Now light wears the robe of matter or materiality. I am sure that this angelic insurrection was within the ultimate plan of the Almighty God, as the material world has become our testing ground—our classroom. For it is through form (matter) that we gain experience and awaken the consciousness. Our challenge, therefore, continues to be our quest for the grail, God's fallen light (Spirit), that hides within all of matter and within ourselves. Frater Ackad tells us:[4]

> *There is a part of the sun in the apple,*
> *Part of the moon in the rose*

Part of the flaming Pleiades
In everything that grows.

Out of the vast comes nearness
For the God of Love, of which man sings,
Has put a little bit of His Heaven
In every living thing.

In general, we are blind to the light and love that underlies matter. We can no longer see the substance that binds the form, its essence. We have, therefore, fallen.

Zoroaster, the Persian religious teacher in the fifth century before Christ, developed a theology of duality between good and evil, light and dark—a theology of separation—that explained the Fall, not unlike the tree that held the knowledge of good and evil in the garden of Eden. Zoroaster (Zarathustra in Greek) taught that there were two powers: Ahura Mazda, the creator of light and goodness, and Ahriman, a slightly lesser power, who fought to destroy the light. The Jews came under this persuasive teaching while they were in Babylonia during the Exile (597–538 B.C.). It was from Babylonia that the Jews received the creation stories that we find in Genesis. But beyond the dualistic teachings of Zoroaster that were partially adopted by the Jews in Babylonia, there was also the Greek philosophy of duality between mind and body, spirit and matter, that had its influence on Hebrew thought.

Prior to these dualistic ways of looking at the universe, Judaism had professed a mystical oneness of all things, where God alone held dominion. In the Torah, the books of Moses that comprise the first five books of the Bible, Judaism was a basically monotheistic religion that left no room for a separate force of evil. In Isaiah 45:7 we hear God say:

I form light and create darkness
I make weal and create woe;
I, the Lord, do all these things.

Judaism calls this dual character of the one God, the right and left hands of God. The left hand of God, a reference from Hebrew scripture, speaks of God as Law, the minister of justice. God's left hand metes out punishment, while the right hand delivers mercy. God was both savior and transformer in the Hebrew scriptures, and for that reason, the name of Satan was used only a few times and rarely as a proper name. Satan acted as the left hand of God. In 1 Chronicles we read about a Satan, while in Job, Satan is called a son of God. Literally translated, Satan is an adversary or accuser, the one who tests us as he tested Job.[5]

St. Paul, a Jew, grew up in the Greek diaspora where he was influenced by dualistic Persian and Greek thought. What we will find, however, is that Paul was far less dualistic than we have become. With careful reading, we can see that Paul, though using dualistic language to describe good and evil, God and the devil, light and dark, is often speaking figuratively, in the Jewish tradition. It is we who have taken the words to be literal and have created Greco/Persian Christianity out of Judeo-Christianity as it was meant to be. Just as Satan was used by God to bring Job to holiness, Paul drew his images from Judaism when he described Satan as the adversary who works with God to bring each of us to holiness. In Colossians 1:16 Paul explains that even the domain of Satan was created through Christ and for Christ:

> For in him all things in heaven and on earth were created, things visible and invisible, whether thrones or dominations or rulers or powers—all things have been created in him and through him.[6]

In 1 Timothy 1:20, Paul suggests turning a member of the community over to Satan that he might "learn not to blaspheme." And in 1 Corinthians 5:5 Paul writes,

> You are to hand this man over to Satan for the destruction of the flesh, so that his spirit may be saved in the day of the Lord.

A parallel perspective is given when Jesus warns Peter that Satan will sift him like wheat.[7] In this passage, Jesus only offers to pray for Peter to be strong; he does not offer escape, for he recognizes that the testing is essential to Peter's growth. Notice that it was the Holy Spirit who led Jesus into the wilderness to be tempted by Satan. And, it is to God we pray, "Lead us not into temptation."

It may seem strange to think of God as an adversary; yet we are not unfamiliar with Yahweh, who punished and who also saved the people. Yahweh is our loving god, a parent and a teacher.

MYSTICAL JUDAISM, when speaking in dualistic terms, believes that it is we who create benevolent and malevolent entities with our thoughts, which then support our actions in either a negative or a positive way. It is these same entities that will then greet us in either heaven or hell. Hell, according to this Hebrew teaching, will last only as long as we need it.[8] Whether this is the case, or whether there are simply entities who roam about *out there,* they are helpless, unless we initiate the thoughts that will attract them. It is we who have given the concept of Satan form. Just as we enjoy creating God in our own image and likeness, our fear has given an idea horns and a tail. And if it is true that we have created benevolent and malevolent entities with our thoughts, then we can exorcise them with our thoughts. All, even the illusion, is for our spiritual growth.

But I do pray daily for protection, even from the illusion, which seems so real. I cast out any spirit of darkness that might have entered during the night. And then I surround myself with the light of Christ for protection throughout the day. When we walk in Christ's light, darkness cannot touch us, for darkness cannot enter an arena of pure Light.

JESUS SAID "FEAR NOT." If there were any real danger he would have warned us. So thank goodness, there is nothing real to fear. Only that which we co-create with God is real. The rest, created out of delusion and darkness through our own imagination, is unreal, and will pass away.

When speaking at a retreat, I sometimes have the room darkened while I light a candle. Then, as we meditate with that candle, we are reminded that all the dark in the world, in the universe, cannot put out the light of that one small flame. Darkness has no power over the light.

Thomas Aquinas said that Light is reality, while darkness is only the absence of light. The world, as we observe it, is here to instruct us, but being temporal, it will not last. Only light and love will endure. In 1 Corinthians 13:8-10, Paul tells us:

> *Love never ends. But as for prophecies, they will come to an end; as for tongues, they will cease; as for knowledge, it will come to an end. . . . when the complete comes, the partial will come to an end.*

Out of darkness, we have created opposites, separation. This duality will be resolved as the roar of the Lion of Judah resounds in our hearts and we remember that we are Beings of Light, who will rise with Christ, the mighty I AM.

> *I AM the great Sun but you do not see me*
> *I AM your husband but you turn away*
> *I AM the captive but you do not free me*
> *I AM the captain you will not obey*
> *I AM the Truth but you will not believe me*
> *I AM the city where you will not stay*
> *I AM your wife, your child, but you will leave me*
> *I AM that God to whom you will not pray*
> *I AM your counsel but you do not hear me*
> *I AM your lover whom you will betray*
> *I AM the victor but you do not share me*
> *I AM the Holy Dove that you will slay*
> *I AM your life but if you do not name me,*
>   *then seal up your soul with tears*
>   *and never blame me.*
>   —Found on a sixteenth-century Norman crucifix

4

The Rise

When we first moved to Boulder, a Christian woman who later became a good friend offered me *The Autobiography of a Yogi*, a book written by the Hindu teacher Yogananda. Having just completed my graduate work in religious studies at Mundelein College (affiliated with Loyola University in Chicago), I told her, self-righteously, that I wasn't interested. With a smile she inquired, "Do you think it could be possible that God has something to teach you that you don't already know?" Wow! And then she continued, "I suggest you pray about it."

The song "The Rose" by Amanda Broom expresses best where my thinking was at that time. The song talks about a heart afraid of breaking, a dream afraid of waking, and a soul afraid of dying. Because of these fears, the song says that we never learned to dance; we are afraid to take a chance. "The Rose" describes exactly where I was in those days. I was afraid to step beyond the boundaries that I had accepted as a child in Sunday school. I had refused Christ's invitation to dance. I had not understood that Christianity is a living organism, not an organization, and that in order to keep pace with Spirit, old thought forms might have to die. I was afraid of waking.

Gradually it became clear to me that there were important concepts that I needed to examine beyond what I had learned.

Slowly my fear left and I began to read the wonderful books, one by one, that my friend gave me. She lived high in the mountains and would lend me only one book at a time. She warned that, otherwise, I might get spiritual indigestion. It turned out to be a summer of timely awakening with lots of trips up the mountain.

That summer I read *The Autobiography of a Yogi, The Cloud of Unknowing, Life and Teaching of the Masters of the Far East, The Way of the Pilgrim, Be Here Now, Cutting Through Spiritual Materialism*, and other mind-opening books. That was the summer when I began to see beyond the confines of denomination as my Christian understanding expanded.

During that time, I allowed, even encouraged, our children to join their friends in different activities in various churches. One daughter returned from a Baptist Bible camp and asked me quite seriously, "Are you and Dad saved?" I assured her that we were (though the Baptists might not have agreed). Another daughter came home one day to declare that she had decided, at age eleven, to become a Lutheran. I suggested that whatever she decided, to do it well. I will concede, however, I was not quite so calm when our fourteen-year-old son decided to tease mom and threatened to join the Hare Krishna movement.[1]

In this smaller world where we live today, it is easy to see that we are becoming a global family. As a family, it is imperative that we learn more about one another, so we can live in harmony. I have come to enjoy the people who knock at my door to share their faith and always chat with the Hare Krishna groups that I meet in airports. Often I am able to say, "Yes, I know Krishna through the *Bhagavad Gita*; he was later revealed as the Lord and Savior of the world in Jesus Christ." Most of these Krishna devotees were brought up in the Christian faith, which allows us to pursue a lively conversation. The amazing part is that I have never missed a plane and one of the young followers became my godchild, though that had not been my intention. On the mystical level, every major religion holds the same truths; for there is only one God called by many names. It is on this level of Oneness that we sustain the hope of unification.

Not only is the world small, but it is changing at an incredible rate. Some see it as a time of devastation, a time that reveals the four horsemen, a time of war, famine, and death. But there is the fourth rider on the white horse, Victory: Christ.[2] I see the present as a time of the final breaking of old forms and a preparation for a new world full of promise. It is late spring and we can be assured the rose will bloom.

Though there is much to learn from the many religions of the world, we can learn first from Christianity. Christ's message of love and forgiveness (reconciliation) is all that we need. Dogmas separate, while love and forgiveness unite. Frankly, it appears to me that the one who simply loves and cares for humanity is often the better example of what it means to be Christian than the more narrow Christians who believe God condemns to hell those who do not believe as we do.

In contrast to that part of each of ourselves that is close-minded, there is a second type of perspective that has no need for a cross, in spite of the fact that the cross has always been central to Christianity. The Lamb of God "who takes away the sin of the world" has become little more than figurative language in liturgical chant. Some Christians today are no longer interested in a god who allegedly required the sacrifice of a firstborn son. I believe this denial is because we have not understood the deep symbolism of the cross.

For this second attitude, we can reflect on the person of Jesus who taught and acted, at all times, with the greatest significance, revealing level upon level of truth. And if we agree to this, it can be suspected that he who manifested divine wisdom in all he said and did, did not die in vain. We can be assured that Jesus did what he had to do, in the way it had to be done, and that his death was part of the integrity of his life.

Jesus chose death on the cross as a dramatic demonstration of who he is and who we are. He showed us that death is not what it appears to be. If he had died quietly in his room, no one would have heard the good news, that Christ lives and that death has no power over us. This message was recorded by the collective unconscious of every soul, those in the body and those out of the body. Resurrection was made possible for all of humanity because of the sacrifice and resurrection of Jesus Christ. Beyond this, Teilhard de Chardin tells us that the planet was divinized with the blood that poured from Christ's side as it seeped into the earth.

JESUS MADE A QUANTUM LEAP from the level of soul to that of Spirit.[3] He became the bridge for each of us to make that same leap. He showed us that death is not real, and that the soul is indestructible. Death is part of an illusion that we experience within the limitations of time and space. But Jesus gave us a way to overcome death, to become Christed Beings. Christ, the Way, lives in us, leading us step by step up the Mountains of Transfiguration, Crucifixion, and Ascension. We are moving from the level of soul to that of Spirit. We must become Christed Beings, because only as Christ are we able to spend eternity in the presence of God. Only as glorified Beings of Light can we participate in the divine life. I recall that St. Augustine said (possibly in his sermons) that Christianity would be successful when in the whole world there was just one Christ loving back God— his father. It is for this reason that we recognize the Christ as the only begotten son of God; for there is only one Christ who dwells in each of us, allowing us to say, I AM.

THE DOMINICAN MONK has an empty cross at the head of his bed. The cross is to be a reminder that we are to hang upon the cross, not because God needs sacrifice, but because we do. Our death on the cross is a dying, a sacrifice, to those things that come between ourselves and God; it is a death to the undeveloped ego. When the ego is truly transcended, there will no longer be a need for physical death. In 1 Corinthians 15:26 Paul tells us that the last enemy to be overcome is death.[4] Jesus died, physically, to give us a complete picture of the Path, which must include death to the lower nature. Had he not come to define the Path, he could have made a quiet transition from this life to the next. But what Jesus accomplished could not remain quiet, for his victory over death joined heaven and earth, God and humanity. Jesus created a cosmic groove leading to physical, emotional, mental, and spiritual well-being. This groove that he created is the Path that leads back to our own birthright, God.

We will continue to experience death until the work of Christ is complete. Even though Jesus said from the cross, "It is finished,"[5] we still find ourselves in a state of sin (ignorance) and separation. In Christ, the redemption that began with the saving acts of Yahweh was finished beyond time and space in the realm of the highest heaven. But the work of salvation must continue on the planet till ". . . every knee shall bow to me."[6] Jesus Christ broke the devolutionary spiral into darkness and confusion as he revealed who we are: children of God. And then as Spirit was poured out, consciousness began once again to rise. Even though the Fall was allowed, God gave us a way back home—Christ—the great I AM.

Christ, the Light of the world, through the life of Jesus, came to show us the way out of this fallen condition back into divine union with God. We shall return as mature sons and daughters, having eaten of the fruit of the Tree of the Knowledge of Good and Evil. We will have tasted suffering and death as we overcome our lower nature and discover Christ dwelling within. Life is a provocative process of becoming who we were created to be.

Together we will move into sanctification that the Kingdom of Heaven might come, and the will of God be done.

HEAVEN AND HELL

God is my joy
My heaven, my home
But hell holds its space
Where often I roam.

Though we believe
'Tis a place where we'll go,
Heaven's not above
Nor Hell down below.

5

The Kingdom of Heaven

*I*n Jean Paul Sartre's play *No Exit,* two women and a man are locked in a small warm room in hell. The three serve as torturers for one another, not with racks and thumb screws but with nervous habits, annoying personality traits, and unkind remarks. There is great conservation of the devil's manpower by this simple method of inflicting pain. It is easy for the audience to see what it would take to turn this situation from hell to heaven, but none of the three is willing to do what is necessary. And that is why they are there. A little love and compassion on the part of any one in the room would unlatch the door of hell and open the gates of heaven.

Each of us holds that key. Each of us can transform hell into heaven. Why is it that we fight as we do against happiness? What is it that makes us hold on to that which does harm? Perhaps there is a sick aspect to the psyche that feels a need to suffer—to be punished. Maybe it comes from guilt. Or is it possible that we are so caught in the world that we are simply lost and cannot find the Kingdom of God, because we don't know where to look?

There is a well-known legend about three old men who looked for a place to hide the Kingdom of Heaven. The first one suggested it should be hidden on top of the tallest mountain, while the second said it could be put at the deepest part of the ocean. But the third and wisest knew that the only safe place to hide the Kingdom would be in the hearts of the people.

We always turn outside ourselves to find, or to create, our heaven. We think that a new situation, a particular person, or a more exciting job will make the difference, while the solution lies, always, within ourselves.

That little story of the three wise men has reminded me of something that happened many years ago in a ghetto church in a notorious part of Chicago known as Mother Cabrini Green. A friend of mine, a nun, played the autoharp and sang there every week. Wanting to hear her, I went one Sunday morning, with several members of our family, to the church. The neighborhood appeared deserted, and as we drove our car near the church we saw that the windows were barred and there were a chain and a padlock on the front door. But five minutes later, the exact time for Mass to begin, the priest, my friend, and about twenty-five parishioners appeared with lots of beautiful children. Together we entered the church, the door being locked behind us. We sang and scripture was read; then the priest gave his homily. He spoke directly to the children so that we might all understand. He began with the question, "What was last Thursday?"

The children all answered with hands waving in the air, "Ascension Thursday."

"That's right," replied the priest, "and what happened on Ascension Thursday?"

Hands flying again, several children called out together, "Jesus went up into heaven."

Then the priest asked, "Do you remember where I told you heaven is?"

One small child, with a question in her voice, answered, "In my heart?"

"That's right," said the priest. "Then if Jesus went up into heaven, and heaven is in your heart, where is Jesus right now?"

All together they shouted, "In my heart."

"Yes. Then if Jesus is in your heart, he is also in the heart of the person sitting next to you. So let's all turn and give Jesus a big hug." And we did. The sermon was over, we clapped. What an incredible teaching we had received!

THE MYSTICS DESCRIBE this inner Kingdom in many ways, but the common factor among their writings is that the Kingdom can be neither defined nor limited. In searching for the Kingdom, St. Bernard of Clairvaux, monk and mystic from the Middle Ages, wrote:

> I went into the higher part of myself, and higher still I found the Kingdom of the Word.
>
> Impelled by curiosity to explore still further, I descended deep into myself, and yet I found him deeper still. I looked outside, and met him far beyond everything exterior to me. I looked within: he was more inward than I myself. And I recognized the truth of what I had read, that we live and move and have our being in him.[1]

When we think of the Kingdom, we often recall the Garden where Adam walked and talked with God. But from that garden humanity was expelled. God stationed cherubim (not fat baby angels, but fearsome creatures)[2] with a fiery revolving sword, to guard the way to the Tree of Life, the God-life within, eternity. Having eaten from the Tree of the Knowledge of Good and Evil, Adam and Eve were denied access to the Tree of Life, for we cannot, mustn't, live forever in a state of separation, duality. When our earliest ancestors chose separation from God, they chose duality, illusion, and death.

Notice that the Tree of the Knowledge of Good and Evil and the Tree of Life are both planted in the center of the garden. One does not need to look very hard to see that there is only one center and therefore only one tree. God has one plan for our salvation. Ephesians 4:4-6 reveals a mystery:

> *There is one body and one Spirit, just as you were called to the one hope of your calling, one Lord, one faith, one baptism, one God and Father of all, who is above all and through all and in all.*

And there is one tree that brings us to Life through the knowledge of good and evil, a tree that is superimposed over the Tree of Life. For this reason, the cross is often called the tree. The cross symbolizes both the trees of death and of life. Having eaten from the Tree of the Knowledge of Good and Evil, we shall return to God. Then we shall eat, again, from the Tree of Life—Christ.

The Kingdom of Heaven is not an experience that awaits physical death but an experience awaiting death to the selfish ego. If we have made God our objective, then everything that happens will be used for that end.

I FOUND THAT EVEN a broken leg can be a gift. A few summers ago I broke my leg because of a silly accident on roller blades. I'm sure you are wondering what this mother of four grown children was doing on roller blades; well, so am I. I was told that I had to spend nine weeks with a brace from the bottom of my foot to my hip before the metal screw could be removed. That was the bad news. The good news was the quality time I had with visiting friends, all that I learned from my condition, and all that my poor family learned! My husband discovered the kitchen and laundry room, while I found how little patience I have, and how I dislike being dependent on others. I have never had so much compassion for those who are house-bound, in pain, and frustrated, to say nothing of the loneliness and feelings of discouragement—and mine was only a temporary condition.

It took me at least three weeks before I could get the accident off my mind and quit counting the days until my leg could bear weight. However, my greatest insight was how strong a connection there is between the physical body and Spirit. I couldn't believe how damaged my prayer life was because of this jarring accident. It was as if my soul were lamenting, "I ask so little of you and you can't even take care of our vehicle." At last, however, we were friends again, my soul and I. The new insights that I received daily would not have come to me if I had been up and about in my usual busy way. It was not long before I could say that I was even grateful for the accident because of the spiritual growth that had taken place with my time to read, think, and pray.

There is not anything that happens that doesn't offer us discovery into ourselves and those around us if we allow it. If we want to live in God's kingdom, it is up to us to recognize and then to allow, through the grace of God, the changes that need to take place in ourselves.

WHEN I WAS A CHILD I thought that the Kingdom of Heaven was a place where I would go when I died. Even as an adult I find the subject a bit confusing. Though we understand that Christ, incarnate in Jesus, brought God's Kingdom on earth, we are still waiting for the Kingdom to arrive as we await the second coming of Christ. Personally, I feel that the time is imminent. In the sayings of Jesus that are found in the non-canonical scriptures, we read:

> *If those who lead you say to you: "See,*
> *the Kingdom is in heaven," then the birds*
> *of the heaven will precede you. If they*
> *say to you: "It is in the sea," then the*
> *fish will precede you. But the Kingdom*
> *is within you and it is without you.*
> *If you will know yourselves, then you will*
> *be known and you will know that you are the*
> *sons of the Living Father. But if you do not*
> *know yourselves, then you are in poverty and*
> *you are poverty.*[3]

This passage seems to suggest that we will find God's Kingdom as we come to know ourselves. For to know ourselves is to know that we are children of the living God. As we allow Spirit to burn away the husk[4] that surrounds us, we will find Christ at the core of our being. We will have found the Kingdom. Paul tells us that:

> *God chose us in him before the world began, to be holy*
> *and blameless in his sight, to be full of love.*[5] *(NAB)*

The fact is that at the core of our being, where Christ dwells, we are holy—perfect. The bridge between the human and the divine has been made firm by Christ Jesus. We need only dare to tread upon it.

AND SO IT IS CHRIST—the hero—who will take us into that higher glory, the Kingdom. We begin by bringing our lives into alignment with the pattern set before us in the ancient mystery schools and then personified in the life of Jesus.

Thus begins the arduous trip into the cave of our own darkness, deep into the waters of baptism, up the Mountains of Transfiguration and Calvary, and then finally we are led out near Bethany to the Mountain of the Ascension. The journey is one of self-awareness, a dying, daily, to our old nature in order to find our true Selves. We will journey now, with the hero of times past, into our own mystery school.

The Mystical Path
(Practicum)

IF YOU BRING FORTH WHAT IS INSIDE YOU,
WHAT YOU BRING FORTH WILL SAVE YOU.
—*The Gospel According to Thomas*

BIRTH

Out of chaos comes order
Out of darkness, Light
From the womb of the Mother
From the blackness of the night

Down deep inside the bowels of earth
One peers beyond that which appears
Into the soul from ages past
Garment upon garment
Fear upon fear

Release each one
Expose the splendor
Of the one so oft reviled
Lying far below the veils
Remembered sadness
Reveals the child

1

The Level of Order:
The Cave Initiation — Birth

*T*he Level of Order is the beginning of self-recognition; for we can't hope to know God without knowing ourselves. And we can't know ourselves until we know God, since we are but an extension of the divine, created from its very essence. So we begin by clearing the clutter from our lives: physical, emotional, and mental. All that stands between ourselves and the Holy One must go.

When we acknowledge that there is something beyond our own mundane existence, we have begun the Path. When we can rise above our chaos enough to call for help, then help will be forthcoming. Because we have been given free will, God will assist us only when we ask, only when we allow a chink in our armor of self-sufficiency. When we open ourselves to the possibility of something that transcends us and this world that we live in, we have begun to prepare for this first initiation. Gradually we will see ourselves, and the world around us, as a part of God's great plan.

THE HERO ENTERS THE CAVE, which was the symbol used by the ancients for the first initiation. When Plato spoke of the shadows on the wall of the cave, he saw a cave where we live in non-reality. The cave is the world that we create with our own limitations, a mere reflection of what is real. As we enter the cave of our being, we invite Christ's light to shine into our darkness, that we might see the shadows. Then we allow the light into the alcoves of our conscious and unconscious minds where the debris of the past is stored.

From the documents of the Second Vatican Council, we are given this insight:

> For by man's power to know himself in the depths of his being he rises above the whole universe of mere objects. When he is drawn to think about his real self he turns to those deep recesses of his being where God who probes the heart awaits him.[1]

The awakening comes with a willingness to change. Healing the unhealthy ego is an uphill battle that must be fought daily, while we rely on the grace of God. As we move along the Path, we will find that the personal ego takes subtle forms. There is a lot of self buried in this cave where we are to be born again.

EARLIER, I DESCRIBED my initial step onto the Path when I was thirteen. However, that experience shouldn't be confused with any one of the five major initiations. As I see it now, that night in Kentucky was a conversion experience that led me onto what I will call the probationary path, a preparation for the first initiation of Order. Though I believed I had given my life to Christ, in actuality I had relinquished very little, for nobody had told me the significance of the cross. Simone Weil, the French Jewish mystic, wrote:

> It was the seed of this tree (the cross) that God placed within us, without our knowing what seed it was. If we had known, we should not have said yes at the first moment.[2]

I didn't know what Jesus meant when he said, "Take up your cross and follow me." I didn't know that I was expected to die to everything that was not of God, everything that was not real.

Though I was young when I had that experience in the hills of Kentucky, I recall being so filled with the love of God that I was ready to undergo any type of persecution or whatever might be asked of me. I often regret the loss of that adolescent fervor. I remember telling the camp director that I wanted to go to the Belgian Congo; I'm sure she smiled at my impetuous decision. The rest of that summer I read stories about Albert Schweitzer and was prepared to sail for Africa where I could really do the Lord's work. I didn't understand, then, that the real work had to begin within my own soul.

The Path is not to be confused with asceticism. We are not talking about rocks in our shoes or burlap underwear. We are talking about becoming aware of who and what we are, which will lead us into an awareness of God.

A Tibetan teacher, Dwal Khul, tells us that it is neither on the path of pleasure nor the path of pain that we will find either wisdom or liberation, but by the transcendence of the two. When we can realize that both fame and shame hold their lessons, we will live beyond the trials of this life.

MANY OF US WHO CALL ourselves Christians have not yet set foot onto the probationary path, have not given our lives to the Christ within. And many of us who have, have not gone beyond that point, to take up the cross. The Path is more than attending church and calling ourselves Christians.

First comes the recognition that we are helpless to manage our own lives. We begin to understand that the only way out of our personal bondage is to surrender to that higher power within which brings freedom. Many will identify this philosophy as the successful doctrine behind Alcoholics Anonymous.

In the days when I relished a martini with an olive, my friend Ruth and I decided we must be alcoholics. So off we went to AA. We stood up and introduced ourselves as alcoholics and then listened for many weeks to the horror stories of those attending the closed meetings. After listening, we found that we were more than uncomfortable sharing our own petty concerns. I even thought of making up stories, or just expanding on the worst incident I could remember.

My husband, who was truly confused by the whole affair, asked me exactly why I thought I was an alcoholic. I explained to him how anxious I was, each evening, to sit down and have a drink with him when I heard the garage door go up as he returned from work. Then he asked me how I felt about a cup of coffee in the morning after my shower. I had to admit that my response to that first cup of coffee was quite similar to the way I felt about a drink before dinner. "Well," he concluded, "You are obviously a coffeeholic."

We were sorry not to be a part of a group that we had truly come to love and respect; but the fact was that Ruth and I weren't eligible. We simply had some bad habits. Knowledge of the "Twelve Step Program," however, made the entire experience worthwhile. It was through that program that I got in touch with some of my compulsive behavior and began to unravel its root system.

Today the AA program is being used for every type of addiction and personality dysfunction. I use it in almost every area of my life. In AA it is on the third step that we abandon our lives to that higher power, a resolve that seems often to work where all else fails. For many of us, however, pride and control issues won't allow us to take that crucial step. Scripture warns against pride when it tells us that only the poor in spirit (the empty) will inherit the Kingdom; for there is no place for the rich (the sufficient) in God's kingdom. Those of us who have all the answers leave too little space for God's grace.

As I have worked to bring my life into order, martinis along with my beloved morning caffeine finally had to go, at least until they could no longer own me. A good friend, Brian, who obviously has a stronger will than I, says that he treats his emotions like his cabinet. He listens to them, but in the final analysis he makes the decisions. I like that.

ON THE LEVEL OF ORDER, we will begin to see God's plan. We will explore the chaos in our lives and talk about what it means to lead a lean life as we set goals. We will recognize the sanctity of God's holy temple, the body. We will discuss what it is to be a disciple. Then we will look deeply into those areas of our lives that need inner healing. As we work with our dreams and our journals we will examine our relationships and hope to bring about balance between the masculine and the feminine within ourselves, to achieve androgyny. And finally we will delve into the subject of suffering and discover that there is meaning in suffering. All of this begins the first initiation on the Level of Order, which is our wake-up call to the spiritual life.

ORDER THROUGH THE PLAN

THE HEBREW WRITERS seemed to believe that God had a plan for each of our lives. In Psalm 139 we read:

> For it was you who formed my inward parts;
>> you knit me together in my mother's womb.
> I praise you, for I am fearfully and wonderfully made.
>> Wonderful are your works;
> that I know very well.
>> My frame was not hidden from you,
> when I was being made in secret,
>> intricately woven in the depths of the earth.
> Your eyes beheld my unformed substance.
> In your book were written
>> all the days that were formed for me,
>> when none of them as yet existed.
> How weighty to me are your thoughts, O God!
>> how vast is the sum of them!

Similarly, Aristotle talked about a plan that was evident everywhere within matter, a plan that held a predetermined goal of goodness and perfection. But we ask, "Within this predetermined plan, where do we have our freedom, free will?"

God has allowed us a variety of experiences on our return Home. When we look at the lives of some of the saints such as

Paul who persecuted the early Christians, Augustine in his *Confessions*, and John Newton, the slave trader who wrote the hymn "Amazing Grace," we see that there is room for all of us in God's plan. These sinners/saints give us hope.

It appears that freedom lies in *when* and *how* the plan will manifest itself. The analogy of the parade where God can see the beginning and end, and all that lies between, is probably a good one. God is the parade master. But the marchers, drummers, and baton twirlers can get out of step, or drop the baton from time to time, while the parade marches toward a predetermined destination.

> *With all wisdom and insight he has made known to us the mystery of his will, according to his good pleasure that he set forth in Christ, as a plan for the fullness of time, to gather up all things in him, things in heaven and things on earth.*
> —*Ephesians 1:9-10*

God's plan is to bring *all* under the headship of Christ. John 12:32 says, "and I—when I am lifted up from the earth—will draw all people to myself."

We were created to love, which is our way back into the Kingdom. However, because we have fear, love does not always come easily. The fact is that we live in a fallen world that has to be *taught* love.

I remember a man who marked the margins of his Bible with the letters E.D. He said they stood for eternal damnation. I showed him how I marked the margins of my Bible with the letters U.S. for universal salvation, which I believe is for all of US, in God's own time. It was the same Bible but with a different perspective.

As we stand at those pearly gates, I believe we will not be asked our denomination, or to what dogmas we hold. I expect only one question, "Have you loved with all your being?"

God's plan *will* prevail. All *will* come under the headship of Christ. Because Christ lives in us, we will find our way home! It is God's plan.

ORDER OUT OF CHAOS

AN ORDERLY EXISTENCE comes with a lean life, a life without clutter. For clutter in our houses, our yards, our offices, and our automobiles is an indication of a disorderly mind.

Once I had a dream about riding my bicycle up a hill. Close behind me was another bike that kept trying to pass, but couldn't. When I looked back, I saw a heavy man on a bike that had fenders, reflectors, a kickstand, and panniers that were overflowing. The man himself wore a coat and long pants. Even in the dream, I experienced a bit of smugness that he would never be able to pass me. But when I awoke, I realized that the man in the dream held a message for me.

How things do pile up! Shoes that were bought in the morning and can't be worn in the evening because of tired, swollen feet. Shirts that looked great in Hawaii. A skirt, or a pair of pants that were bought on the condition of losing five pounds. Old tires, one stereo speaker, a dog house without a dog, and the list goes on. Some of us still have our high school cheer-leading outfits hanging in moth balls next to the felt skirt with the poodle and chain.

My situation wasn't quite that bad; but it was bad. So I began to go through my closets, attic, garage, and all the places we collect those many things that *we might need some day*. I forced myself to throw out and give away anything that had not been used or worn in two years. What a relief! Granted, there are times I miss something, but I have no real regrets. I remind myself that pilgrims travel lightly.

When we realize that we must dust, repair, insure, dry clean, rearrange, have pride in, and worry about losing these many objects, we wonder about the advantage of owning them. The pilgrim is expected to be ready to fold the tent and move in the middle of the night when God calls. Life is not to become a burden, neither because of our accumulated material objects, nor the objects of our minds.

ABSTINENCE FROM NOISE, such as radio and television, is part of the uncluttered life. For a balanced life we need to be aware of things going on in the world, but we do not need background noise that might block the voice of God. Who knows when the Lord might want to speak to us? What a shame if we have obstructed that voice with unnecessary noise and a cluttered mind.

It is impossible to do real work on the soul in the midst of confusion and turmoil. A look at our social or work calendars will give us a quick insight into our priorities. There are times when my calendar looks like a New York Times crossword puzzle that has been worked and reworked—in ink. Just what am I doing with my days? I forget that a truly productive day can be spent looking at a flower. I needn't feel guilty about my re-creation time.

Sometimes we fool ourselves about what we are doing. We might think that because we work in an office, we are not doing God's work, while those who visit a nursing home, organize the church bazaar, or volunteer at the food bank, might feel they have earned stars in their crowns. However, it is not what we do, but how conscious we are while we are doing it. Do we have what is called a horizontal relationship with God when we are with friends, neighbors, family, and co-workers? Are we aware of Christ in ourselves and in those around us no matter what the outer appearance might be? If we are unable to recognize Christ in each one we meet, it is because we have not yet found the Christ within ourselves. This discovery will happen in our vertical time with God: prayer time.

It is the quiet time, preferably in the morning, that makes the difference. If our lives are too busy, even though it is what we see as worthwhile work, it is simply an excuse, an escape from God. It is an awesome thing to come into the presence of the living God, and many of us spend a lifetime avoiding it.

We need time that is set apart just to get to know God. God time is a time when we come together to hear the Good News. It is time for study of the written word, holy scripture. It is a time to sing and to praise God. It is time in silence for listening.

And eventually it becomes a time when we are continually aware of God's presence.

As the clutter is moved out of our lives, we gradually begin to realize that there is no longer a separation between the sacred and the profane; for all is holy, all is sacred. Work is no longer an escape, since all is filled with God's presence. My favorite writing on this subject is by the Sufi Abū Saīd:[3]

> If men wish to draw near God, they must seek Him in the hearts of men. They should speak well of all men, whether present or absent, and if they themselves seek to be a light to guide others, then like the sun they must show the same face to all. To bring joy to a single heart is better than to build many shrines for worship, and to enslave one soul by kindness is worth more than the setting free of a thousand slaves.
>
> The true saint sits in the midst of his fellow men, and rises up and eats and sleeps and buys and sells and gives and takes in the bazaars among other people, and marries and has social intercourse with other folk, and never for an instant forgets God.[4]

Our intent is to be ever aware of the presence of God in all we think, say, and do. Awareness takes practice. In the beginning, we need consciously to set aside time to be alone with God. We protest, "But I don't have time for daily prayer and study." Then we need to examine our priorities.

Dag Hammarskjold, past Secretary General of the United Nations, was asked by a reporter how he managed to do all he did in a given day. He replied that he couldn't possibly do his work without the hours he spent each day in prayer and meditation.

IT IS GOOD, ON THOSE DAYS of new beginnings such as birthdays, to reevaluate our use of that precious commodity, time. The time that is set aside each morning will actually make the rest of the day seem longer. Time spent with God will instill in us peace and a sense of well-being that causes the day to slow down as we become aware of each moment. There is a time to say "yes" and a time to say "no." The quiet time spent at the beginning of the day will increase discernment throughout the day as we make these decisions. Time with God gives us perspective in our lives and allows us to plan, to set goals, which gives meaning to our lives.

ORDER THROUGH GOAL SETTING

GOAL SETTING IS PART of an orderly life, because there can be no organization without some semblance of a goal. The goal may be only for the next hour, or for that day, but goals assist in bringing about a clarity and motivation that doesn't allow life to slip through our fingers. For that reason we also set long-term goals. A friend, Del Anderson, says that we must first desire the goal, then believe we can reach it, act as if we can, and be willing to let go of the habits and negative attitudes that keep us from the flow of Spirit.

The ultimate goal is reunion with God. But to aid us in that noble intent, there is a particular blueprint for each of our lives. We can discover that plan only by listening to God, letting our souls affirm what we hear, and then setting our strategy into action. Our goals, however, must never be so concrete that they don't allow us to move when Spirit says, "Move."

In setting goals, it is helpful to see where we have been, so we can see better where we are going.

MY FIRST EXPERIENCE with goal setting was in a Matthew Taylor workshop where we were given a large, elongated piece of paper on which we drew a line from one end to the other. Then we marked the line with increments of time in years, or groups of years. Beginning with birth (or even conception), we then moved forward with our biographies.

We started with the years before school, then the years of schooling that were mixed with travel, sports, and meaningful people in our lives. We were told to record such things as illnesses, accidents, and other traumas that had occurred during that period. I didn't realize the impact this data would have until when I reached age seven on my big piece of paper, I noted that my parents had divorced. I also noted, in that year, that I had received a sweet little white kitten named Sugar that everyone blamed for the onset of my allergies. Looking at that time line I realized, for the first time, that the divorce probably had more to do with the allergies than the kitten.

After recording the years of my early childhood, I moved into adolescence, then dating, college, work, marriage, rearing children, and on to the present. Then the facilitator asked an unexpected question, "Now what will you do with the rest of your life?"

The answer turned out to be, "Just about anything we might want to do." At that point we sat quietly, listening to our inner guidance. As we listened, we observed what excited us, or motivated us, and wrote it down. At the same time, we attempted not to interfere with the process as we released our preconceived notions and limitations. Step by step, a plan began to emerge from our latent dreams and desires. Then a structure was built around the dream that gradually became quite concrete. Finally, there was the decision to act, to do it. The German writer and philosopher Goethe (1749–1832) spoke of the hesitancy that is present until one is committed to a decision to act. But he noticed that when the decision was made, Providence moved in and things began to happen that would otherwise never have happened. He suggested that one ought to step out in faith knowing that in the acting, we can expect the unexpected as assistance comes from above.

Though many of us feel called to a given work, few of us have prepared ourselves. And now we say, "I am too old, I don't have the time, the necessary funds, the energy." But if it is God's plan, then all the resources will be there for us; we need only tune in and then follow that inner leading. With God, all things are possible.

Next our workshop leader told us to look ahead and to ask ourselves, "How many years will I live, and in what kind of health?"

We insisted, "But I have nothing to say about any of that."

The instructor countered, "Not true!" He told us that we are responsible for our lives; we are not victims. Then he talked about the power of the will and that we are meant to be co-creators with God.

That day I began to try to focus on the ideal, believing that I could help to create it. I reflected on the scripture, "As a man thinketh in his heart, so is he."[5] I vowed not to limit my thinking, but to think big!

As WE SET OUR GOALS, our lives will begin to take direction, order. Goal orientation does not negate the ability to live in the moment. In fact goal setting releases us to be even more spontaneous. Setting goals gives us a tranquility that enables us to be at peace without concern for the future. When we have our minds set clearly on Christ and can see the plan for our lives, our lives will take on order and purpose.

We rise early to sit in the silence, listening. The day begins with joy and power. With quiet time in the morning alone with God, all else falls into place. Now we can hear that inner voice throughout the day as we are guided in our activities. We eat lightly and properly, exercise moderately, and breathe deeply of God's love. We are beginning to understand that we do have something to say about how long we will live, and even in what kind of health.

ORDER THROUGH A HEALTHY BODY

IN ORDER TO ALLOW more Light to generate in us and to flow through us, we need to cleanse the body from the skin all the way to the marrow of the bone. According to Dr. Candace Pert, the cells of the body record every life experience. We are not only what we eat, we are what we see, hear, read, dream, and do. We are constantly in the process of programming the body, the emotions, and the mind. And what we have put in can be the dickens to get out.

By looking closely at the body, we have some idea about the state of the emotions and the mind of a person. Often a trauma or a poor self-image is carried in poor posture, an underweight, overweight, or an unkempt body. Losing unnecessary fat, gaining needed weight, or getting stronger, can be conditioning for the psyche and the emotions, as well as for the body.

To build a suitable temple for Spirit, we start by eating properly. Depak Chopra, M.D., talks about the amazingly short period of time that it takes the cells of the body to replace themselves. So we can say, frequently, that we are brand new. The question is, "Of what am I made this month?" If the body were an automobile we would never dream of pouring Pepsi into the gas tank. But we test the body's ability to perform each day with food and drink that, if we operated like an automobile, couldn't get us out of the garage. Proper diet is essential to the spiritual path.

When Daniel and his friends were invited to eat from the king's table, they refused, which led to their being tested. The steward allowed them to eat only vegetables and water for ten days, as he waited to see the deterioration of their bodies.[6] We all know the rest of the story. They thrived. Daniel was acting on instructions received from God.

Many athletes, especially runners, have found that eating only vegetables, fruits, and grains builds the strongest bodies with the least illness.[7] Notice that it was only after the Fall in Genesis that meat was suggested for consumption.[8] Prior to that time, God said:

> *See, I have given you every plant yielding seed that is upon the face of all the earth, and every tree with seed in its fruit; you shall have them for food. And to every beast of the earth, everything that has the breath of life, I have given every green plant for food.*
>
> —*Genesis 1: 29-31*

Even the animals were not meant to be carnivorous. We await that time when the "lion shall eat straw like the ox" (Isaiah 11:7).

For those who take medication, eat meat, refined sugar, dairy, and drink caffeinated and alcoholic beverages, an occasional fast is beneficial. The cleansing fast that I use is: Two and one-half cups fresh lemon juice to one gallon of distilled water. To this mixture I add one teaspoon cayenne, as a blood cleanser, and enough grade B pure maple syrup[9] to sweeten the beverage.

I drink as much and as often as I desire, while I rest and drink purified water to help remove the toxins. Some form of mild laxative, such as an herbal tea with senna, taken each evening while on the fast, also facilitates the cleanse. Three days seems to be a good length of time to clear the system, depending on the severity of the pre-existing condition.

Moderate exercise and pure water are as important for purifying the cells as the food we eat, or don't eat. Clean water flushes the system of impurities, while exercise pumps air into our lungs refreshing the blood. Because of all the pollution in the water and air today, we are well advised to drink distilled or filtered water, and to supplement the diet with antioxidants, herbs, and vitamins. A health store consultant should be able to advise us about these dietary supplements. If we keep the body healthy, disease will not be able to find a home.

More and more of us are turning to alternative health care and to preventative medicine. Today many types of body treatment have become common, such as massage that rids tissue of toxins; rolfing that realigns the body by manipulating the connective tissue giving us better posture and therefore better health; acupuncture that can relieve pain and inflammation; and chiropractic adjustments, which have often been maligned because they are misunderstood. In the fourth century B.C., Hippocrates taught, "Look well to the spine for the cause of disease."

The spine is the seat of the central nervous system, and misalignment of the spine can be the source of many physical, emotional, and even mental problems. We tend to think that misalignments in the spine are caused solely by physical trauma.

Emotional stress, however, can be equally devastating. Either trauma, physical or emotional, produces a torsion or stretching of the spinal cord that can result in shock to the central nervous system. When the spine is adjusted and we move into proper alignment, not only do we feel better but our responses are more appropriate, since the body has been able to release the chemical, physical, and emotional traumas that are held in the cellular memory.

WITH PRAYER, PROPER DIET, exercise, and therapy, lifelong negative patterns will gradually break down and then shift into positive patterns as more light and life are able to pass through the body. Spirit relies on soul, soul relies on the body, and all rely on God. It is up to us to furnish God with a body that can be used for the building of the Kingdom. Rarely does one think about the fact that our journey to God goes hand in hand with our physical body, whether it is standing, or in a wheelchair.

> There is but one temple in the universe, and that is the body of man . . . we are the miracle of miracles—the great inscrutible mystery.[10]
>
> —Thomas Carlyle

With our physical lives beginning to come into order, we are now ready to become disciples—to lead more disciplined lives.

ORDER THROUGH DISCIPLINE

I LOVE MONDAYS, New Year's Day, Advent, Ash Wednesday, a new moon, and birthdays. These are all beginnings that allow us to restructure our lives. Over the years I have put myself through periods of various types of discipline. I have fasted, abstained from meat and drink. I have read my Bible obsessively, meditated, attended daily Mass for a time, and performed acts of charity. During these times I have found myself feeling virtuous when I have managed to hold to the vow, and filled with remorse and guilt when I have failed. As I look back, I think that what I did, when I did it, was good, and that each time I learned something from it. But there is a discipline beyond all of these.

The highest discipline is a response to a plea from Christ to live consciously, keeping "oil in our lamps."[11] Discipline is listening to the heart. Discipline is "washing our robes."[12] Discipline is the practice of living in God's presence at the center of our being. Discipline is celebrating life, moment to moment.

When Jesus called disciples to himself, he didn't call those who were perfect; he called those who were willing to be disciplined and changed. It is encouraging to take a look at the erratic behavior of the group that Jesus chose for his apostles. Except for John, they all failed to show up for the crucifixion, and most lost heart until Jesus appeared to them after his resurrection. But then, with the guidance of the Holy Spirit, they pulled together to lay a foundation for the largest single religion in the world.

I have often asked myself what kind of disciple I would have been. I wonder if I would have recognized Jesus as Lord if I had lived when he lived. And then I wonder if I would have deserted him as the others did. Then I ask the real questions, "Have I recognized Christ and the call to discipleship today? Am I willing to take on Christ's yoke and learn the lessons that I need in order to be a worker in the vineyard?" And I ask, "What does it really mean to be a disciple?"

In Matthew 24:42-44 Jesus tells his disciples how they must await his second coming:

> Keep awake therefore, for you do not know on what day your Lord is coming. But understand this: if the owner of the house had known in what part of the night the thief was coming, he would have stayed awake and would not have let his house be broken into. Therefore you also must be ready. . . .

This scripture instructs a disciple how to act at all times. Again, in the garden when Jesus admonished his apostles to "stay awake," he was giving instruction that went beyond that night in his hour of trial. And he says to each of us, "Stay awake."

In *One Minute Wisdom* by Father Anthony de Mello there is this delightful dialogue:

> "Is there anything I can do to make myself enlightened?"
> "As little as you can do to make the sun rise in the morning."
> "Then of what use are the spiritual exercises you prescribe?"
> "To make sure you are not asleep when the sun begins to rise."[13]

The sun is beginning to rise and many of us are asleep. If we do not think, speak, and act at all times with integrity, with the mind of Christ, we are still comatose, still caught in the illusion that surrounds us. For not only our actions but also our motives must be pure. In fact, the motive is far more important than the action or spoken word. We must stay awake, conscious of our thoughts, feelings, and even our pain, in order to hear God's voice. The difficulty will be with our nature, which has a tendency to get lost in our thoughts and activities. It is not easy to stay present to the Eternal, since our thoughts tend to dwell on yesterday or fret about tomorrow. We are dreamers, lost in the past and the future, while God dwells in the now.

When we lose awareness of God's presence, we think and act in ways we later regret. There is hypocrisy in what we say we believe, and how we respond to real life situations. Our lives are disparate, disconnected. There is no continuity, no order.

So we enter the cave of our darkness with the light of Christ to discover what it is that keeps us from being able to live at the center of our being.

IN BRINGING OUR LIVES into order through discipline, we examine the motives behind our thoughts, our feelings, and our actions. We ask, "Why do I do what I do? Why do I experience feelings of guilt, failure? Are these feelings legitimate?" We examine the root of the feeling or emotion. "How do I feel with certain people—doing certain things? Why?" We set aside months to record our responses and reactions to every significant situation in that time frame. We begin to know ourselves and to change.

A detached attitude is beneficial at this time of introspection. When I have worked with this exercise I have called myself by name as if I were a separate being. My Higher Self then has a dialogue with my personality. As I reflect on a circumstance I say, "Betsy, you were truly upset by what happened. Why?" Then I look within to recognize the source of my reaction. I ask Christ to reveal the cause. If the cause can surface, then the opportunity is there for healing. When I look deep within, I often find that the cause is a wound from my childhood that keeps me from reacting appropriately in times of stress.

In another circumstance, I might say, "Betsy! Why were you showing off?" Curiously the answer is often the same; it is woundedness that has left a poor self-image. When we recognize in ourselves what lies behind our actions, we tend to be more forgiving of ourselves and of others.

After only a week or two of this careful observation, a pattern starts to emerge. We are able to identify procrastination, denial, stubbornness, anger, hurt, deceit, and many other mental and emotional disorders. Interestingly, we will find that most of these negative reactions are reflections of the same missing part in our lives, a part that was deprived of love or of proper discipline, which is a form of love.

In order to be a true disciple, we must make the decision to remove our defenses. We may need help in recognizing these defenses, but after we acknowledge them, the many disguises that protect us will begin to crumble.

This self-protection, which we have taken a lifetime to reinforce, has been built to shield us from authority figures, those whom we consider to be above us, and from those we think are beneath us. We like to believe that we are not class-conscious. However, if we have put anyone above ourselves, including the Pope, or a king, or the president, we operate within a system that pigeonholes people. We believe some people to be inferior to us, while we see others as superior. We have judged. We have failed to recognize Spirit within another, and we have believed power to be external.

I thought that I no longer had a problem with categorizing people and idealizing celebrities until I was recently put to the test. My husband Bob and I were visiting the home of a friend who is a congressman in Washington. His wife was out of the country, so I was alone in their house most of the day. About ten o'clock one morning, I answered the phone to hear, "This is operator number one. The President would like to speak to Congressman Porter." I almost jumped up and saluted. Obviously I wasn't "awake" when the phone rang; for there is no awe of another when we are Christ-centered. When Christ speaks to Christ, neither is impressed nor condescending.

IN ANCIENT GREECE, above the entrance to the oracle of Delphi, one could read, "Know thyself." And Plato taught that the unexamined life is not worth living. It takes discipline to examine ourselves. Having fallen asleep a long time ago, we lost the knowledge of who we are and what we are about. We have banded together with those who accept us, those who act much the same as we do, which makes us appear to be okay. But there is a higher heaven to which we can aspire. Someone once said that every human contact is an opportunity to expand or to contract. Only in love can we expand.

Love comes gradually as we learn to know and to love ourselves. St. Teresa of Avila stated it plainly in the *Interior Castle*:[14]

> It is absurd to think we can enter Heaven without first entering our own souls—without getting to know ourselves. . . .

Some will say that self-examination is egotistical. In response, we ask, "Do we not need to practice those boring scales if we want to play the piano? Does the athlete not work out day after day in order to build the body?" It is when the fingers are strong and move easily with each note that we can forget the scales. And it is when the body is well developed that the athlete can ignore the body and compete effectively. In the same way, it is when the lower self is purified and made whole that the personality can be forgotten.

We tend not to see the similarities between the successful musician, the athlete, the person in business, the scientist, and the individual who is on the Path. But all these have a common bond—hard work and even suffering (carrying the cross). When we take our God-given talents, add God's grace, and then strive to develop our gifts, the secular and the sacred will come together, even if we don't recognize that the work is ultimately spiritual. Whenever we direct our energies toward the development of the mind, the emotions, or the body, there is progress toward building a proper vehicle for Spirit. We can see that many are preparing for the Path at this time, even though they appear to have no spiritual awareness.

IF A CHILD IS NOT brought up with love and discipline, then the school takes on the job of developing the personality. Where the school fails, the peer group will often teach the necessary lessons. When our peers fail, discipline can be taken over by the military, a job, friends, a spouse, our children, in psychological counseling, or maybe not at all in this lifetime. But self-awareness desperately needs to take place, for again, knowledge of God comes only with self-knowledge. The process requires persistent self-examination. There is no time to doze off into the world of illusion.

Moment-to-moment awareness sounds impossible; but when we think of the work as a celebration of life in every moment, then awareness becomes joy. When we are aware, we give thanks for all things. When we bless, we are blessed in return. Unbelievable things begin to happen as we move deep within.

ORDER THROUGH INNER HEALING

AS WE BECOME SELF-AWARE, we will begin to notice things about ourselves that are no longer acceptable, things we can't seem to control, actions and reactions that come from lost memories. This recognition will lead us into the hidden memories from the past, that they too might be revealed and healed.

Solving problems is like stringing pearls without a knot in the string when we haven't dealt with the underlying causes. Healing of the memories, a technique developed by Agnes Sanford in the fifties, is an excellent method of psychic (soul) healing.

Mrs. Sanford, a Christian teacher and writer, claimed to remember being somewhere on a heavenly plane when a "Being of Light" came and asked her if she would be willing to come to earth to teach the healing of memories. She said she distinctly remembered saying "no." However, she must have changed her mind; for she came and shared that powerful teaching with those who were ready to hear.

Agnes Sanford described a time in her life when she entered into a deep depression. As she surveyed her life, she could find no reason for not being happy. Yet she was deeply troubled by something that she couldn't define. She began to take an inventory going as far back as she could remember. As she traveled through her life, year by year, she wrote down the things that bothered her. Each week, when she approached the altar in the Episcopal Church to receive Holy Communion, she handed an envelope containing a year's confession to the priest, who then burned it. After many weeks, Agnes completed her life inventory and the depression left. Through her tedious introspection she found healing.

From this personal experience of depression, Agnes built a method of inner healing that employs a guided meditation. The meditation can be done with a friend, a minister, in a group, or by oneself. In some cases, the prayer might take many sessions, but each session will relieve the petitioner of some burden. Even though we say, "But I still suffer from the same old problems," these are not the same old problems. Once we have handed a problem over to Christ to be transformed, there is a change. We might fail to see the change because the healing isn't complete on all the levels: physical, emotional, mental, and spiritual. But the pain from our past that we have handed over to our Higher Self, Christ, is healed on some level if not on all levels. The memories may not be forgotten, but they no longer hold their sting. We seem somewhat more removed from our past and more able to look at it objectively, which, in turn, heals the present.

CONTINUING WITH THIS first initiation of the hero, we move deeper into the cave of our birth. We cannot expect to live holy lives in the present moment until we have dealt with the past. Sometimes this healing entails a journey back even to the moment of conception, where the cave becomes the womb.

Was this tiny baby conceived in love, or did the conception take place on the level of lust? If the latter is the case, then we must ask healing from the seeds of self-doubt that were planted by the unconscious parent or parents at that time. If we were not planned or wished for, then we may have felt a sense of rejection and even guilt deep within our psyches. We should not think of this ill-conception as a sinful deed—and certainly it is not one deliberately directed toward the unborn child—but as an act performed out of ignorance.

Remarkably, during this prayer for inner healing, we may even recall the emotion that surrounded our conception and the feelings that accompanied the womb experience. The first time I was led through the healing of memories, I realized that my birth was considered a mistake by my parents. And even if I had been desired, I was the wrong gender. I, therefore, had deep feelings of rejection. Later, when I began to analyze the situation surrounding my conception, I realized that my mother and father were in their forties and were actually contemplating divorce at that time. My father chose to punish my mother by ignoring me for years. I was not aware of how much sadness I had repressed until I began these sessions of inner healing.

The second time I was led back into my childhood, I was asked by the minister to pick up my father and to place him in the arms of Christ for healing and forgiveness. In my imagination I had picked him up and was walking toward Christ when suddenly I became furious and dropped him on the floor. Then, in my mind, I just turned and walked away. That act gave me great relief and was probably appropriate for that stage of my healing. It was many years later that I was able to understand and to love my father.

Too often I see people who allow the circumstances of their childhood to continue to influence their adult lives. There comes a time to say, "That's enough, now I will get on with my life!" It takes a mature person—or a little child—to forgive. The ability to love and to let go comes through God, and it is to God that we appeal for the grace to perform this divine act. The fact is that forgiveness cannot take place in heaven until we forgive on earth because those things we bind on earth are bound in heaven (Matthew 16:19). And until we forgive, we cannot be forgiven. It is God's law. Only in forgiving can we be healed, forgiven. The choice is ours. We can hold on to bitterness; or we can let go and experience the freedom that comes with that loving act of pardon.

The place for the unveiling of the innermost self is in the company of God's Spirit. Unless you have experienced this healing of memories, it might seem implausible. I assure you, however, that it works. We can never underestimate the power of God to respond to prayer.

THERE ARE TIMES, however, when we are so filled with hurt or shame, that we are unable to pray, which is usually the time we need prayer the most. We have given the sin (an act of ignorance) far more power than it deserves. We don't need God when we appoint ourselves judge, jailer, and executioner. The real sin is our failure to reconnect with the divine. When we allow a shadow to fall between ourselves and God, we have disconnected ourselves from life itself. When we have failed to forgive, we have denied love, and without love we wither and die.

Many years ago, I regularly visited an elderly doctor who was blind. One day he told me about his grandson, an accomplished pianist, who suffered from schizophrenia. Being inspired by what he told me, I promised him that if I were ever given the opportunity, I would visit his grandson. About a year later I happened to be in Washington D.C., so I went to St. Elizabeth's Hospital where the young man was a patient. I did not know if there was even a chance that I might be allowed to see him. However, much to my relief, the staff members were open to my visit. The doctor in charge of the case talked to me and prepared me for the anti-social behavior that I would encounter.

I proceeded to a ward with about eight young people, all schizophrenic. I settled myself in a comfortable room that had a ping-pong table, some game tables, and a television. The television was not properly set and the picture was flipping from frame to frame while several young people sat on a sofa watching the flipping pictures. Others wandered around the room, mostly staring at me. The person I was there to visit managed to avoid me though I spent several hours trying to get his attention. At one point, a girl seated herself across from me and started to laugh. So I laughed. She began, "I hope you don't mind if I laugh, but you are funny looking." I laughed even harder. Then she became quite serious and asked hesitatingly, "Do you think I am funny looking?"

I sensed in her that deep need to be accepted, loved, I replied honestly, "I think you are beautiful, truly beautiful." Very quietly she got up and left the room. About fifteen minutes later she returned. She had turned her blouse around (it had been backward) and was brushing her hair. Again we talked. This time she did not laugh but seemed more able to reason. We actually had a pleasant conversation.

How we crave love and long for someone to see our beauty, for we are truly beautiful. Each of us is an attribute of God. Once we begin to discover the goodness within ourselves and then start to manifest those attributes, we can help others find who they are. So aside from those who suffer from severe mental illness (we all suffer from some), we need simply assure ourselves that we are here for a reason as we attempt to discover what that reason, or virtue, might be.

We are also given the opportunity with each one we meet to help that person love him- or herself. You or I could be the one to turn a neglected life toward self-love, true mental and emotional health.

I heard that when Mother Teresa was asked by a young person what one could do to make a difference in this suffering world, she replied, "Just smile."

HOW WONDERFUL TO BE ABLE to say, "I am loved, I am forgiven." Or even, beyond that, to feel like one who has never sinned. For when God forgives, the slate is wiped clean. In God's eyes, it is as if the separation never occurred, as if we had never erred; for love does not brood over injuries (1 Corinthians 13:5).

Some have found, however, that though forgiveness can be accepted with the intellect, the heart is not always moved. Sometimes the heart hurts too much. Mrs. Sanford learned from her dramatic experience that only Christ, in a gentle and loving way, can heal the damage that has been done deep down inside the soul.

So we invite Christ (who is inhibited by neither time nor space) to be present at our conception, to be with us in the womb, and to be near at the moment of our birth. Then we ask that the source of those feelings of rejection and self-hatred be revealed. The healing begins when we can identify the origin of our insecurity and hurts. For some, it is a comfort to invite Mother Mary (in our creative imagination) to hold that wee infant, to rock it, sing to it, and tell it how much it is loved. We are to be reminded that we are created in the image of Love, that we are Love. Lastly, we must address the memories that we have unleashed, for they will now rise to the surface.

These memories will return only as fast as we can bear the pain. One at a time, they will come to be healed. We move from infancy, through childhood, into our school years, relationships, work, and on up to the present moment. When we find we are stuck in trying to recall the past, that might be just the moment of awakening.

There are also experiences, so painful, that the mind protects us by burying them beyond our ability to recall them. In such a case, we must ask for healing of that which we are unable to remember. We observe our behavior, and recognize that there have been hurts and abuses that must have been incredibly severe. Or perhaps they were sins of omission; we were never loved. It is possible that, having never been truly loved, we are not even aware that there was something missing from our nurturing. In that case, we must look closely at our own ability to love. Is our love free, unqualified? Does our love hold conditions? Do we love only when it is deserved? Meister Eckhart (1260–1329) preached that it is wrong to love any one human being more than we love any other.[15]

In the beginning, we love only as much as we have been humanly loved, but we are not limited forever by that experience. The love of God can be taught to us; and then it begins to seep into our soul as we are healed. We are beginning to be able to love and to be loved.

Inner healing will continue as we seek androgyny, the balance between the masculine and feminine qualities within ourselves.

ORDER THROUGH ANDROGYNY

I REMEMBER, AS A freshman in college, being given a sheet of questions pertaining to things that did or did not give us pleasure. As is often the case in introductory psychology classes, it turned out that we were to provide the statistics for some graduate student's thesis. Our answers to the questions were then tabulated in order to tell us what percentage of our psyches was considered to have masculine traits, and what percentage had more feminine qualities. That was the beginning of my awareness that women are not one hundred percent feminine and that men are not one hundred percent masculine. Now I can say "Thank God" as I have come to realize how incompatible we would be with the opposite gender if that were the case. Later I read the writings of Carl Jung and found androgyny to be a fascinating study that is vital to our coming to wholeness.

So God created humankind in his image,
in the image of God he created them;
male and female he created them.
—Genesis 1:27

The very image of God is androgynous—male and female—Mother and Father.

It appears that we are all born with a sexual orientation that can be observed on a spectrum. If we use the numbers one to ten with one representing (what we call) female behavior and ten, male behavior, most women would fall somewhere between one and five, while the majority of men would fall between five and ten.

1___2___WOMEN___3___4__(5)__6___7___MEN___8___9___10

As we become more whole, more complete, men and women are moving toward the number five where we will be able to have fuller lives without the limitations that have previously been imposed on gender.

ACCORDING TO GARY ZUKAV, in his book *The Seat of the Soul*, families have always been either patriarchal or matriarchal, which has shaped the lives of children. In the days of either strong patriarchy or matriarchy, children did not learn to be both male and female; they learned how to be male or female. But the time has arrived when men and women are integrating their masculine and feminine attributes as we move toward a much needed balance in the individual, a higher form of evolution. Carl Jung called this balance "androgyny." In the Jungian system, a woman needs to discover her rational side, which is considered a male quality, while a man needs to develop intuition, a feminine trait. Neither quality, just as neither gender, is inferior to the other.

Remember, it was after the Fall that God said to Eve concerning Adam, ". . . and he shall rule over you." Female submission to the male is part of the fallen condition. In one of his more enlightened moments, Paul wrote to the Galatians:

> *There is no longer Jew or Greek, there is no longer slave or free, there is no longer male and female; for all of you are one in Christ Jesus.*
> —*Galatians 3:28*

We can conclude that submission is to be reserved for the Christ in each of us. Man is to humble himself to the Christ in woman, while woman humbles herself to the Christ in man.

In *The Kingdom Within*, John Sanford[16] shows how Jesus was an androgynous being with perfect balance between his masculine and feminine counterparts. Jesus could deal with multitudes, a female quality according to Jung, while his male aspect sent him into solitude in order to gain inner strength. Sanford pointed out how Jesus cleansed the temple with a whip but wept when he approached the tomb of his friend Lazarus. He chose twelve men to follow him, though he had strong ties to many women. A man could lay his head on Jesus' breast, and he spoke softly to children. But he could turn and make scathing remarks to the Pharisees. Sanford gave many other examples to suggest that the masculine and feminine qualities of Jesus were integrated as they ought to be.

PRIOR TO THE SECOND WORLD WAR, a man was seen as the sole breadwinner, while women stayed home with the children. Even as late as the 1960s, I remember the time Bob came home from work and found a tripod in the center of the kitchen floor dripping grape juice into a pan. Three of our little ones were making grape-juice prints on the linoleum and the white cabinets. Bob took one look at the disaster and left. I learned later that he went to his mother's house where he was treated to a steak dinner. At that stage in my life I didn't know that his behavior was unacceptable, nor did he. In the 1960s, we were only beginning to question our roles. Men were still men and women were women, which was to say that men were free and women were not.

Though the blending of roles really developed in the 1970s and 1980s, it began during during World War II when men went to war and women went to work in factories and in offices. Women began to discover that they could make ammunition and decisions as well as they could change a diaper. The war and its widows marked the beginning of the development of the masculine (more rational) side of women, which eventually compelled men to discover the feminine (intuitive) side of themselves as they joined with their wives to care for the home and the children.

It seems that young people today are entering marriage with a healthy understanding of themselves and of their position in the family. Divorce was the popular expression of freedom in my generation, while the baby-boomer generation seems to have recognized the damage they received because of that phenomenon and are taking better hold of their marriages. I read recently that the divorce rate is now sixty percent, but I have also read that seventy-five percent of all first marriages last, which would suggest that many of the divorced keep getting divorced. It appears to me that those marriages that are solid are based on respect and a sound understanding of mutual responsibility. Today, young fathers are more nurturing toward their children and are less threatened by the talents of their wives. These healthy psyches even find it acceptable for the wife to work while the husband stays home with the children.

More and more, we are beginning to recognize that we are human beings who can gracefully exchange predetermined roles without losing our image of male or female, mother or father. In fact, many children today are benefiting from quality time with both parents, partly because families are now smaller. We see that it is possible for each parent to have well-integrated masculine and feminine traits that will be handed to their children. If these attributes are properly developed in the parents, they will be properly developed in the child. It goes without saying that the time spent with our children in their early developmental years is critical.

Someone once said, "The best gift a father can give his children is to love their mother." And then it is equally important for a mother to show this same love to the father. The fifth commandment that was given to Moses by God was:

> *Honor your father and your mother, as the Lord your God*
> *commanded you, so that your days may be long and that*

*it may go well with you in the land that the Lord your God
is giving you.*

—Deuteronomy 5:16

A psychologist might translate this into: "If you grew up with respect and love for both your parents, your chances of having a healthy psyche are good, and you are therefore more likely to live a long and prosperous life." This is the gift that we want to give our children.

In order to continue the quest for androgyny and self-understanding at a deeper level, we will now enter the kaleidoscope of our dreams.

ORDER THROUGH DREAM WORK

INTERPRETING OUR DREAMS is perhaps one of the most helpful tools we have for understanding ourselves on this Level of Order. Insights are given to us during the night that we often pass over during the day. Since we are unable to face our own reality directly, we dream in symbols. We say, "I can't remember my dreams," or "I don't dream," but without the release of stress and the unveiling of problems in our dreams, we would lose our sanity. To remember and to try to comprehend these dreams is extremely important.

Before we go to sleep, we pray to be able to remember our dreams. And then we pray for help in interpreting them. We begin with a notebook next to our beds so we can jot down key words from our dreams when we wake during the night. This can even be done in the dark. If we fail to make even a cryptic note, we will probably not remember the dream the next morning. We will also find that if we wake in the middle of a dream, we can ask to return to it, and often we will. If we do wait until morning, and cannot remember a dream, we can sit in a chair, close our eyes, and ask the dream to return. The more we try to force ourselves to remember with the rational mind, however, the more we push the dream away. As we pray to remember, we are assisted by those who watch over us, the angels.

According to Carl Jung, everything in the dream is a part of ourselves, including the tree, the hole in the ground, the small animal, and on and on. In our dreams, we sometimes encounter our animus, the masculine counterpart of the female, or our anima, the feminine counterpart of the male. The anima and the animus are Latin terms that were used by Jung to describe the hidden elements within each of us that are needed for androgyny. This one we meet in a dream, who represents the animus or anima, is always of the opposite gender, and usually a person we do not actually know. A man could have a dream where he meets a beautiful woman. They could sit in a meadow, feel a warm rapport, touch, kiss, or even make love. Upon waking, the dreamer might feel something akin to bliss. Throughout the day he would feel supported, loved. That would be a dream in which the dreamer has met his anima, or feminine counterpart. A dream of that sort is not to be interpreted as lust. We know the difference. The tenor of the dream will tell the dreamer its meaning. The dreamer's interpretation of the dream is the bottom line. No one else can have the same intuitive feeling about the symbols and deep levels of meaning, as the one who has had the dream.

Often dreams speak to us from ancient archetypal images. These are figures that have existed from early times in myths and in fairy tales. The frog (one awaiting transformation), the apple or the wicked witch (bringer of evil), a wall around the castle (impediments), a path (opportunity), or a baby (a new beginning) are all archetypal impressions. We find these images in cartoons as super heroes who are archetypes of evil, justice, or power. Or one might say, "My mother is an archetypal mother," meaning she epitomizes everything about motherhood. These archetypal images are the ancient and obvious symbols that occur in our dreams and give us insights into the interpretation of a dream.

People have told me that they have dreamed about me, and then they proceed to counsel me according to the dream. It is not easy to say to the dreamers that they are only discovering an aspect of themselves. Instead, I ask, "What do I represent to you?" In interpreting a dream we always ask about these projections, "What does he, she, or it, mean to me? How do I describe that person, or that object? Can I see myself in that person, or that object? Do they have a quality that I either admire or find objectionable?"

For many years I dreamed about houses, not knowing at that time that houses are full of symbols to help us discover ourselves. Each level in the house represents some part of our being. The basement can be the unconscious mind that holds the collective unconscious (universal mind),[17] or it can be all the things we have repressed, or it can simply have to do with a gut feeling. The lower level can also represent our lower nature, our animal instincts. The main floor might symbolize the conscious mind or everyday mundane affairs, though it could have to do with the heart, the very core of our being and our feelings. The attic or upstairs would be the highest level of consciousness, the mind or the spiritual realm. The precise significance would depend on the feeling that accompanies the image. The house dream, or maze, can be traced, archetypically, to the labyrinth that Daedalus built on Crete for King Minos. At the end of the maze is a minotaur ready to devour the dreamer. The minotaur, like everything else in the dream, is a part of ourselves that can tell us what we need to know, if we are willing to confront it. When we confront the beast (ourselves), we usually avoid being devoured.

My house dreams offered me a house full of closed doors. Fear would creep in, as I opened one door after the other; I would wait to be frightened at best, and devoured at worst. The fear became greater with each door. Just as I opened the last door, terror would wake me before I was able to see what was inside. Finally I received some insight into these nocturnal extravaganzas that made me realize that I must confront what was behind the door, or around the corner, or in the hidden place.

When we are taught how to confront that hidden part of ourselves in a dream, it is amazing that we can actually remember, while dreaming, the instructions that were given to us. It is also interesting that the revelatory dream will occur shortly after we are prepared for the confrontation. We will find that lucid dreaming[18] allows us to be so calm that we can even ask the intruder if he or she (sometimes a monster) has a gift for us. The gift will give us the insight we need into our hidden self or, at precious moments, into our Higher Self.

The intruder might hand us a box containing one of any number of things: a heart (we need to feel a situation), a golden ring (fidelity), a tree (life), a rose (Christ or Mary), or any of many hundreds of symbols. The meaning behind the symbol will be clear, because it will be so personal that we will know immediately how it applies to us. Once we understand the message of the dream, we will probably not dream that dream again.

Sometimes the dream will reveal our shadow, the underlying cause for the negative aspects of the personality. In the second movie of the *Star Wars* series, "The Empire Strikes Back," Luke Skywalker asks Yoda what he will find in a dark, dank hole in the ground that is filled with snakes and other similar creatures. Yoda, the sage, replies that he will find only what he takes with him. Skywalker jumps into the pit (the unconscious mind) and finds Darth Vader, the epitome of evil, who is dressed in black. Skywalker confronts his own dark shadow and they begin to have battle. Then Skywalker, with a swift movement of his sword of light, whacks off Darth Vader's head. As the helmet rolls back, it reveals the face of Skywalker himself. *Voilà!* Luke discovered that the fearful creature in black was himself—his own fear.

IN ONE OF MY many house dreams, I was hanging up wet clothes in the basement when I heard footsteps upstairs. Having been coached on what to do, I was able to be conscious enough to realize, even in the dream, that I must have a meeting with this entity. I waited at the foot of the stairs as the heavy steps descended one by one. I was terrified. At last a man appeared. It was our milkman, but strangely he was black in the dream. I know the appearance of our milkman at the foot of the stairs doesn't seem like much of a teaching. However, the fact was that at that time I had a strained relationship with the milkman. I would forget to put out a note and then end up with enough milk for the entire neighborhood, or no milk at all because I wouldn't remember to bring in an old note; so I had canceled our milk delivery. This jolly man had suddenly turned hostile and had written me a really nasty letter about what an ungrateful person I was. From that time, I had avoided going out my front door until I was sure he had made his rounds. I didn't even like to think about him. And there he was at the foot of the basement stairs in my dream.

In the beginning, I was sure this was not a significant dream, but I wrote it down anyway and tried to understand it. I asked myself, "What does this dream tell me?" The most obvious symbol was the fact that in the dream he was dark, an aspect of my shadow, or buried side. Otherwise, at first glance, the interpretation seemed fairly obvious. I had an unfinished relationship with another human being. We needed to reconcile our differences, and in fact that opportunity did arise a month or so later. But the dream held another revelation. I was washing clothes, which might signify my own "dirty linen." I was in the unconscious level (the basement) of my mind, washing my own dirty linen. Next I had to think about the milkman. What did he represent to me? I thought about his personality, which had usually been entertaining. And then I realized that was not the truth about who this man was. He was entertaining as long as I bought the milk. But when I was no longer his customer, he became decidedly hostile. He was two-faced, a hypocrite.

Could an element of that hypocrisy possibly be in my own personality? The answer was obviously yes. And then I proceeded to try to recognize this aspect of my character. Was I truly honest in most of my relationships? No. I wanted people to like me. Could I be honest? It would be painful. So I began to make daily notes in my journal of how I felt and reacted in the midst of interactions with various friends and acquaintances. I wrote down when I was dishonest—a phony. Next I began to try to see how I could change without hurting anyone; for it isn't necessary to be rude just because we have decided to be honest.

Over the years I see that I have been able to change somewhat because that dream made me aware of a part of my personality that I had not been able to see. The problem, when I examined it, stemmed from a basic feeling of insecurity, a need to be admired and loved.

Facing ourselves is never easy, but if we want to grow in Spirit, we must. What I uncovered, in that dream, was only a portion of my hidden darkness. Dreams still come, nightly, to reveal more and more of myself.

In a recent dream I was aware that our house was on fire. I seemed to be alone and danger was not imminent. I went first to the family pictures and decided to leave them. Then I went to where we keep all the important household records, and decided not to bother with them. After the filing cabinet, I went to a secret place where, at times, I have hidden jewelry, and decided that was not important. Finally, I went to the back yard, climbed up on the fence and watched our house burn to the ground with no feeling of remorse, even though I have truly loved our house for the twenty some years we have been in it. That was a very revealing and encouraging dream about my attachment to the things of the world.

The Lord will continue to show us to ourselves, if we are willing to try to remember our dreams and to work with them. Dream work is too complicated to be done alone, or without some training. I had the good fortune of meeting, once every two weeks for several years, with a group of women and a dream teacher, Barbara Pellouchoud. We shared our dreams and tried to help one another interpret them. Because a dream is so personal, it is often difficult for us to have insights into our own dreams. It is the forest and the trees problem. Often others can see what we cannot, but still our own interpretation is the last word. We must be totally open and honest when we do this group work.

As we continue to avail ourselves of the teaching within the dream, our dreams will become clearer; we will remember them better and be more able to recognize the symbols. Good dream work is one of the most fascinating and fun ways we can come to wholeness. Ideally, the work is done with a Jungian psychologist, but this may not be geographically or financially feasible. So we do the next best things: we read, we attend classes, and if we are fortunate, we find at least one or two friends with whom we can share our dreams. Because our relationships will become extremely intimate as our dreams reveal our deepest secrets, these friends will become the ones with whom we feel safe as we share our joy and our suffering.

ORDER THROUGH SUFFERING

JUST WHEN WE THINK we have our lives in order, often a tragedy will occur. Everything seems to be thrown out of balance and our lives move back into chaos. How can we cope? Is life still worth living? Why? Why? Why?

Viktor Frankl, psychiatrist and survivor of a Nazi concentration camp, wrote: "If there is meaning in life at all, then there must be meaning in suffering." But we resist finding any meaning when we are so totally destitute. I remember the movie "Oh, God" with John Denver and George Burns, who played God. John Denver asked God, "Why do you allow all the suffering in the world?"

God replied, "Why do you?"

SUFFERING IS AN OUTGROWTH of the Fall and is a part of our lives because we have chosen to separate ourselves from the perfect will of God. God does not cause suffering but allows and uses it. Just as the body uses nerves to point out which area of the anatomy needs attention, mental or emotional suffering is used to point out what part of the psyche (soul) needs attention. Without the nervous system we could do irreparable damage to our bodies, while psychological pain directs our attention to that part of our lives that we have not yet surrendered to God. Suffering comes in many forms, but the one we are particularly concerned with here has to do with emotional suffering that comes, most often, from a wound to the ego or from a loss of those things we hold dear.

Nothing creates more questions for us than does this subject of suffering. We ask ourselves, "Why, if God is good and all that God made is good, is there torment and heartache in the world?" It may sound presumptuous to say that we will try to comprehend this question, but we will. We will enter deeply into the wound of suffering to examine it and even, perhaps, to understand it a little better as we return to the Fall.

AFTER HIS FALL FROM HEAVEN Lucifer no longer had one mind with God. He had developed a mind of his own. The ego of Lucifer revealed its egocentric (separate) state in the writing of the prophet Isaiah (14:13–14):[19]

> *I will ascend to heaven;*
> *I will raise my throne*
> *above the stars of God;*
> *I will sit on the mount of assembly*
> *on the heights of Zaphon;*
> *I will ascend to the tops of the clouds,*
> *I will make myself like the Most High.*

Lucifer now had an independent nature from God, a will of his own. He had used his free will to become separate from the perfect will of God.

Adam represents a progression of the story of Lucifer. Adam sensed his separation from God long before Eve's deception. Though he had walked and talked with God, he had lost his oneness with God and was lonely. He yearned for companionship, so God gave him woman.[20] Adam and Eve sought the lost union with God in their own physical union, which gave them no lasting satisfaction. There was still a feeling of loss, of estrangement. Influenced by the Luciferian mind of separation, Adam and Eve ate from the Tree of the

Knowledge of Good and Evil in order to be like God, knowing all. They were then sent forth from the garden—the Kingdom of Heaven—where they would grow in that knowledge, painful as it might be.

Now we move to Job who carries forward the story of Adam, of fallen, suffering humanity. Because of our inability to deal with hardship, we have interpreted Job as saying that tragedy falls into the realm of the absurd, that God is unreasonable and that suffering is not meant to be understood, only endured.

I cannot believe, however, that God would have given us the gift of free will, knowing that it would create suffering, unless it had some purpose. And while the rest of Hebrew scripture speaks of the justice of God, is it not incomprehensible that a just God would be frivolous with Job, and with us?

To study the condition of Job is to take a further step into the understanding of the way of the cross—the path of the mystic—a path back to God.

It has been said that there is no coming to consciousness without pain. Job is the example *par excellence* of this conjecture as he suffers physical and emotional loss. It is in understanding Job that we can understand our own suffering a little better.

In the book of Job, Satan is the adversary who tests God's servant in a complex situation where Job appears to be above reproach. Job's friends recall the law of retribution where we reap what we sow and suggest that if Job were without sin, he would not be in this plight. But Job continues to maintain in the beginning:

> I am clean, without transgression;
> I am pure, and there is no iniquity in me.
> —Job 33:9

First, Job is tested concerning his attachments to family and to material wealth. All of his material possessions and his children are destroyed. Job passes the test as he is able to say:

Naked I came from my mother's womb, and naked shall I
return there; the Lord gave and the Lord has taken away;
blessed be the name of the Lord.
—Job 1:21

The second test is more direct as it affects the actual physical well-being of Job. His entire body is covered with boils. Again he could say, "We accept good things from God and should we not accept evil?" (Job 2:10)

Now comes the third, and most subtle trial, personal criticism. Humiliation comes to Job because his friends continue to question his righteousness. For seven days, Job sits with his three friends in utter shame, and at the end of this time he curses the day he was born, though he continues to protest that he is without sin:

Until I die I will not put away my integrity from me.
I hold fast my righteousness, and will not let it go;
my heart does not reproach me for any of my days.
—Job 27: 5-6

Job is a proud man. He is proud of his goodness. He is proud of his position at the gate of the city where wise men sit each day to discuss weighty matters and to bring judgment on sinners. But we recall from Proverbs 16:18 that

Pride goes before destruction,
and a haughty spirit before a fall.

So we await Job's fall.

But now they make sport of me,
those who are younger than I,
whose fathers I would have disdained
to set with the dogs of my flock.
—Job 30:1-2

We no longer hear him saying, "The Lord gave and the Lord has taken away, blessed be the name of the Lord." Instead he disdains those who have chastised him. Job could withstand physical loss, economic loss, and even the loss of his children, but he could not stand the loss of his reputation, especially with those whom he held in contempt. Job could live with the boils, but not with the question of his goodness, not with shame. The sleuth has uncovered the tragic flaw in Job, pride. But it is the young man Elihu who reaches to the core of the matter.

Elihu speaks in Yahweh's defense. Though young, he upholds his right to speak by telling Job that understanding does not come with rank or age but with the spirit in man. He says that God makes his ways known in dreams and visions and that he chastens with physical suffering. He declares that the Almighty cannot violate justice, and that we are totally dependent on God:

> *If he should take back his spirit to himself,*
> *and gather to himself his breath,*
> *all flesh would perish together,*
> *and all mortals return to dust.*
> *—Job 34:14-15*

In other words, everything in life is reliant on God, since all of creation is imbued with God's Spirit. God is Law (justice) and Grace (love); God is all that is. After Elihu's eloquent introduction, the Almighty speaks from the whirlwind, showing Job how ignorant he is concerning the heavens and even the earth. God tells Job that he cannot be saved by his own right hand; he can be saved only through grace. Job is humbled. He recognizes that his mere obedience to the law has not been sufficient, for he had not truly comprehended God. He repents, allowing God to be God, and union is complete.

We are reminded of the passage in Ezekiel where God warns that "the sleek and the strong I will destroy." God has destroyed the pride of Job that there might be holy union. We reflect again on the words of Paul, who said, "I hand him over to Satan for the destruction of his flesh so that his spirit may be saved on the day of the Lord."

Job was a self-righteous man who felt that to follow the law, as he understood it, was salvation. He failed to include himself in the fact that "all have sinned"[21] even though he admitted "Who can bring a clean thing out of an unclean?" (Job 14:4). Like most of us, he could not see his own dark side. In not recognizing his shortcomings, he set himself above others. Failing to identify his shadow, he was unable to repent. But he was a holy man who desired righteousness and for that reason, he was purged by Satan (the left hand of God) until the breakthrough was made.

THOUGH THERE ARE numerous passages in scripture that suggest a connection between sin and disease, we cannot say that all illness is an outcome of sin. I do know, however, that the body, mind, and emotions are intrinsically related. Unconsciously we have all used an illness to get out of an obligation or simply to be able to rest for a while. Often the mind and body work together to accommodate us. God doesn't create illness or an accident, but on the other hand, God has no better way to get our attention than when we are flat on our backs. When we are ill, especially if the illness is considered to be quite serious, everything takes on a different meaning. Suddenly the things that were important are no longer important, and the things that were unimportant are important. We all know how an accident or sickness can change our lives, sometimes for the better, if we allow the good to emerge. The body and the mind work together to help bring us to wholeness.

Much of the work that was done by Sigmund Freud dealt with what he called hysterical or psychosomatic illness. In such cases, when the psychological problem was discovered and healed, health was restored.

A young man named Michael, whom I have known for many years, was a hot dog (acrobatic) skier. He loved skiing and was tempted to follow the circuit around the country doing just that. But as much as he loved to ski, he felt that he had been called by God to work in the school system to encourage young people to build a good self-image which would enable them to say "no" to drugs and other ignoble activities. But he could not make the decision to give up skiing and to get on with his vocation. Then one day, while skiing, his knees simply collapsed under him. The doctors could find nothing wrong, but he was temporarily unable to ski, so he began making arrangements to work in the schools. Some time later, he was skiing again with his old buddies, listening to their glory stories, when he began again to get excited about the ski circuit. As he and his friend were getting off the lift, suddenly Michael's knees buckled under him and he had to be taken down the mountain in a sled. Back home his legs were as good as new. His body had repeated its message. It seemed to Michael that his conscience was speaking through his body. He now enjoys skiing from time to time but is devoted to his work with young people. He feels fulfilled as he uses his gifts to answer what he believes to be God's call. His work in the schools is built around his artistry on the trampoline, which (not surprisingly) has never caused his knees to buckle.

IF WE SAY, "I have no suffering in my life," we are saying, "I have little compassion," for one cannot read a newspaper without entering into the suffering of the world. Yet there is no suffering that does not hold a lesson. The lesson is there for us if we are able to find it. And once we recognize the teaching, the agony will diminish and then pass away, for it will be there only long enough to instruct us. The length of time, however, may be unto death—the ultimate healing.

But death also causes suffering. It is odd how we, who think of ourselves as spiritual or religious, have such irrational fear of this crossing over that we call death. I hope that one day soon, death will again become a celebration as it was in the early church. I am sure that what we call death is considered to be a birth in heaven. I imagine that the angels and saints celebrate our passage from death to life, just as we celebrate the birth of a baby.

Most of us want to believe that death is a simple transition from the life we see to the life we are unable to see, and that the soul cannot be destroyed. Furthermore, who are we to say that a certain death is untimely? God, being just, will resolve whatever is unresolved. It is our clinging that causes the suffering. We cling because we are not whole and we have refused to allow another to be whole. We *need* our spouse, our children, a parent, or a friend, because they make us whole. When we can allow another to be fully who they are, even allow them to suffer and to find their own way, then we can find our own way. I believe that once we accept that there is no death, that life continues in the way that is best for us, suffering will be eliminated. This is not to say that we will not mourn, but we will be "comforted."[22] It is time to live as though we believe the promise of heaven, otherwise we dare not call ourselves believers.

BEYOND INDIVIDUAL TRIALS, there is collective suffering for which we prefer to claim no responsibility. There is planetary suffering that we must all endure because we have polluted the air, the water, and the earth. There is national suffering that we have brought about through neglect of certain groups that often results in dereliction, street crime, or civil conflict. And there is suffering from wars caused by stupidity and greed. In the Second World War the Japanese made weapons and planes from the scrap metal we had sold them. And in the Persian Gulf War, Iraq used the weapons and the strategy that the United States and its allies had given them during the Iran–Iraq war. People are starving, not because of insufficient food but because of a criminal mentality that blocks the flow of food. We suffer because we are ignorant of the fact that we are not only our brother's keeper, but we *are* our brothers and our sisters.

AGAIN WE ASK, with Viktor Frankl, what is the meaning behind suffering, or is there any meaning?

I am sure that each of us can think of a situation of suffering that appears to have no redemptive value. We ask God, "Why do you allow all the suffering in the world?"

And again God replies, "Why do you?"

The subject of suffering is our link between the physical (order) and the emotional (will). There is still the suffering of an unconscious world where we are called to participate in the redemptive act of Christ on the cross. We are called to enter into the suffering of those around us; just as Jesus took on the sins of the world, we are to "bear one another's burdens."[23] We are to weep with the sisters of Lazarus. We, like Christ, must become one with the suffering of all mankind while maintaining that inner peace and tranquility that flows like a river through our being. As we begin to see the bigger picture, we will eventually learn to transcend suffering. God's Kingdom will come on earth when we can see with the eyes of Christ. But first we must empty ourselves and give back to God the gift of free will.

FREE WILL

He watched as she left
He knew she would return
But he was sad
And the Boy wept

It was harder than she
Had thought it would be
The days were cold and
The nights were lonely

Yes, she was free
But it wasn't what
She had anticipated
Her soul longed for Spirit

From time to time she
Felt she had found him
But she would awaken
And find it was only a dream

Then the Boy came
And offered her his life
She didn't understand
She turned away

Time passed
The Sun drew near
The dawn grew brighter
And the night turned to day

He held her in his arms
And on the seventh day
They did rest
The Boy was glad

2

The Level of Will: The Stream Initiation— Baptism of Water

$\mathcal{T}$he Stream Initiation (sometimes called Secret of the Sea), represents the emotional or feeling nature that is symbolized by water. Having received an introduction into the feelings and emotions on the Level of Order, we will now examine them more closely on this Level of Will.

Throughout history, there has been a movement back and forth between periods of romanticism and science (the intellect). During those times when the head took precedence over the heart, feelings were considered to be a feminine and undesirable trait, while reason was left to men.

Today, we understand the need for harmony between the head and the heart in both men and women. Though the intellect allows us to move into this age of science and technology, it is through the heart that we come to know God.

I often hear from the pulpit that we don't have to like someone, but we have to love them. We are told that love is a matter of decision, a matter of the intellect. But it seems to me that those who say this do not know the passionate feeling of real love. No matter how many intellectual decisions are made, if there is no feeling heart, there is no love. We are fooling ourselves when we say we love someone we don't like. The fact is that once we like ourselves, we will love/like others.

The water initiation, the most difficult of all the initiations, will heal these difficult emotions. When the emotions are cleansed, the other initiations will then fall into place. After this level, we will be free from the things that have obstructed us on the unconscious level. We will be free to love. We will be able to live in this moment, asking God for our daily bread (manna), while we seek forgiveness for our transgressions of this day. Our past will be healed.

THIS LEVEL OF WILL is expressed in Jesus' water baptism, which was followed by his temptation in the wilderness. The wilderness experience was an appropriate extension of this initiation, which is full of tests. Notice that Jesus was led into the wilderness (by the Holy Spirit) to be tested by Satan.[1] Again we see the left hand of God. This initiation is a test of the emotions, our desire nature. Satan tried to appeal to the desire nature of Jesus as he offered him power. Jesus, however, was able to transcend those base desires. He chose the cross—death to his lower nature—the path of the mystic.

I have read that baptism, at the time of John the Baptist, was often a terrifying experience. John's baptism was to bring about purification and reform for the sake of the Kingdom. He baptized Jew and Gentile alike.[2] If it is true that John was from the Qumran community where the Dead Sea Scrolls have been found, then it would not be surprising that baptism was a very serious, if not perilous ordeal. The Essenes were an austere, yet zealous people who lived asceticism to the extreme.

In the sixth chapter of Paul's letter to the Romans, baptism is seen as a death that brings resurrection:

> Do you not know that all of us who have been baptized into Christ Jesus were baptized into his death? Therefore we have been buried with him by baptism into death, so

that, just as Christ was raised from the dead by the glory
of the Father, so we too might walk in the newness of life.

The death that is spoken of here is a death to the ego and the desires of the ego. There is a story about the Buddha in the sixth century B.C. that reminds us of John the Baptist and the teaching of Paul on the severity and meaning behind Christian baptism.

A young man came to the Buddha seeking enlightenment (salvation). Buddha took his disciple into a lily pond near where he lived. After they waded into the pond to some depth, the Buddha grasped the young man, struggled with him, and then held his head under the water until the man had almost ceased to resist. Then he drew him out of the water. As the disciple was still choking, the Buddha asked him what he wanted more than anything else when he was under the water? The young man gasped, "Air."

"When you desire Nirvana (Buddhist heaven—salvation) as much as you desired air, then you shall have it," was the Buddha's reply.

IN THE BAPTISMAL SENSE, water is meant to cleanse the soul. But baptism is not just something that happens to us once; it is something that we are to experience daily as the layers of self-deception and self-deprecation are washed away.

In 1984 my husband Bob and I were in Israel, where we were baptized in the Jordan River. When I told my parish priest about our experience, he was thoroughly displeased and informed me that we didn't need to be baptized because we had already been baptized. I reminded him that I had now been baptized three times—once as a teenager in the Christian Church, when I was immersed; then by the Catholic Church, because they weren't sure that my first baptism was valid; and then in the Jordan River. Now I understand that I am baptized daily, as I change daily.

Though my elderly priest was not open to my many baptisms, the Roman Catholic Church today teaches that baptism of water is not necessary for salvation. In fact Catholic doctrine allows for three types of baptism: baptism of water, baptism of blood that was achieved by the holy martyrs, and baptism of desire such as we see in the thief who hung next to Jesus on the cross. The thief repented and was accepted into heaven by Jesus. It seems to me that in the case of all three of these baptisms, there was a great desire, as in the community's desire for a baby to be baptized. Water was merely the symbol of the emotions and of the cleansing that was experienced through the desire to be purified.

Contrary to this more liberal interpretation of baptism, there is the case of a neighbor who told one of our children that those who had not been immersed in water were bound for hell. In hasty response to my distraught child, I picked up the phone and called her. I asked what she thought about the baptism of fire that is spoken of in Matthew.[3] She replied, "That is obviously not to be taken literally." What more could I say?

I remember when Catholicism relegated unbaptized babies to a place they called Limbo, a doctrine which I never did accept. It appeared to me to be poor theology in the light of a loving and just God. The idea of Limbo is no longer spoken of and is now an embarrassment that Catholics would rather forget. I assume this revision was made retroactive for all those little unbaptized babies.

Even though I am convinced that the sacraments are imbued with divine grace and power, I have never considered that one needed to be dunked or sprinkled to enter heaven. The idea of baptism extends far beyond the earthly elements, which of themselves, are powerless. It is the desire for purification and reform that saves.

WHEN JESUS WASHED Peter's feet at the Last Supper, he said, "Unless I wash you . . . you have no share with me." Then Peter asked the Lord to wash all of him, to which Jesus replied:

> *One who has bathed does not need to wash, except for the feet. . . .*
>
> —*John 13:8-10*

This passage, in connection with the general washing of feet at the Last Supper, has often been interpreted to mean that Jesus called us to serve one another, which is true. However, scripture most often reveals more than one level of meaning, and it is obvious here that more is intended. For example, we know now that the feet hold neural connectors to every part of the body, making the washing of the feet a symbol of the physical, emotional, and mental ministry that we have to one another. Also, the word for bathed in "the man who has bathed" has a Greek root that is used in a baptismal context throughout Christian scripture[4] just as the washing of the feet was connected with baptism in early Christian liturgy.[5] The passage continues, "you also ought to wash one another's feet" (John 13:14). So we can conclude that we are to have our own feet washed and to wash others' feet in a baptismal sense. We are to minister to one another. This washing begins a process of purification and forgiveness that moves us from the mundane to the divine. As we wash feet, we are washing the under-standing (more than a pun).

We ask, "Of what are feet made? What is the foundation upon which I stand? What is my understanding?" We can only learn the answers to these questions from those around us. Only in community do we really test ourselves.

There is a story about a desert father[6] who went to the abbot and said, "At last I believe that I have reached holiness." "Good," replied the wise abbot, "Now go to the village, find work, marry, have children, and interact with your neighbors."

COMMUNITY CANNOT DO its job unless we allow ourselves to be vulnerable, allow others to wash our feet. What submission it takes to expose our bunions, hangnails, callouses, crooked, and sometimes even smelly feet. As we discover ourselves, we become aware that we judge in others what are our own short-comings. These deficiencies are so well hidden in ourselves that they have become our dark side or shadow that we project onto others. Sometimes the only way to find our limitations is to look carefully at what we judge in others, since we can see ourselves best in and through those around us, the mirrors of our soul.

We will begin the second initiation with the discovery of our desire nature, a gift from God.

WILL AS DESIRE

SPINOZA, THE SEVENTEENTH-CENTURY philosopher, wrote, "Desire is the very essence of man." Desire was the gift that came to us in the same package with free will. Free will allowed us to wish for and to desire things within and apart from the perfect will of God. Desire allowed us to depart from God's plan. This is much the same gift we give our own children when we let them leave home to pursue their own desires and to learn from their own mistakes.

God allows us our desires even when they are not in our best interest. We are able to pursue our dreams and our nightmares. Though we are still part of the parade, we don't have to keep step. Desire may lead us astray, but it is more constructive than apathy. Scripture tells us that the lukewarm will be spit from the mouth of God.[7] It is essential to develop an ego—a personality that can express our gifts and follow our desires. Otherwise, we will not grow; there will be nothing for us to give back to God. We are like the man who buried his pieces of silver and was scolded by the master when he returned for not having invested them.[8] It is better to invest our treasures (our gifts) and learn from our mistakes, than to hoard what God has given us. Desire is our curse and our blessing, our fall and our salvation.

Some time ago, when I was giving a workshop for a group of Catholic women, a member of the group said something about having free will, so I asked her when she had received it.

"At birth," she replied.

I questioned, "Did you choose your parents?"

"Well, no, how could I?" (I actually believe that Souls do choose their parents, but I didn't say anything.)

"Then when did your own will begin to operate?" I asked.

By then the entire group was involved in the discussion and one participant suggested that we receive free will at age seven when we first receive Holy Communion.

"At seven you were truly able to make a free decision?" we challenged.

After much banter back and forth we decided that we were not free to make our own decisions at that tender age. Even if we try, it is rare to make a decision of the will that is not programmed into us by our parents, our friends, our teachers, and all those who influence our lives. Or a decision is sometimes a rebellion against the program, and that is not really a free decision either. It sounds paradoxical, but our true freedom comes when we give back our gift of free will in order to come under the divine will of God.

The philosopher Hegel[9] said that a truly free will is "enlightened by understanding and guided by reason." Ultimately, that is a will that operates within the divine will of God. It appears that God gave us free will as a loan; we are to give it back, with interest. In Matthew 11:25, Jesus taught that what God has hidden from the learned and the clever, has been revealed to the merest children. Only when we can have the abandon of a child, do we allow Spirit to guide us in the decision to attune our will to God's will. Ceanne DeRohan has written:

> When the Individual Will feels the loving acceptance of its own Spirit, it cannot fail to come into alignment with the Divine Will.[10]

Desire becomes aspiration when we desire to align our will with the will of God. Only then are we free.

WILL AS EMOTION

THE LEVEL OF WILL examines and distinguishes among emotions, feelings, and intuition. The purification of the will moves us from reactions that are connected to the emotions, to feeling and thinking responses that come from the heart and the intellect. Again, feelings are our connection to God. It is by nourishing our feelings that we awaken the intuition. We will gradually become feeling/thinking people who are no longer crippled by emotions. As the emotions are transformed and transmuted, they will move from the solar plexus (gut), to the feeling level of the heart, where we will become effective co-creators with God.

I realize that distinguishing between feelings and emotions may be little more than an exercise in semantics, but it is one that has helped me assess my own passions. As I see it, the will expresses itself, ideally, as feelings. On the fallen level, however, will is expressed as emotions that react, most often, in defense of the ego. A person with feelings can be detached from the feelings, while we tend to think of an emotional person as one who is possessed by the emotion. Most of us would prefer being thought of as a feeling rather than an emotional person. Emotions interfere with our thinking processes, to say nothing of the fact that they do not allow us to hear God, who speaks quietly to the listening heart. When we are centered in God, there is a calm in the midst of chaos or even tragedy.

In the autumn of 1991, before I had made this distinction between feelings and emotions, I had a semi-private visit with the Dalai Lama in New York City. I asked him if he considered anger to be a legitimate emotion. He replied, "Yes, it is a valid emotion, but it must never eclipse reason." And then, with his assistant, he tried to recall when he had last been angry. The Dalai Lama was sure that it had been within the last three years, but his aide countered, "Your Holiness, I can't remember you ever being angry."

Perhaps anger that doesn't eclipse reason doesn't look like anger. The anger or emotion to which we are accustomed is in defense of the ego, as opposed to righteous anger, which is in defense of truth. Because we tend to react instead of respond to most situations, we fail to recognize or to understand a proper response when we see it.

A good example of righteous anger (as opposed to self-righteous anger) was Jesus' cleansing of the temple.[11] We picture Jesus acting as we might have acted in a similar situation, with anger. But nowhere in scripture does it say that Jesus was angry; instead, the incident recalls Psalm 69:9, "It is zeal for your house that has consumed me." Jesus was about his "father's business."[12] He made a whip of cords with which he drove sheep and oxen out of the temple area. Yes, he knocked over the money-changers' tables, but there is no mention that he was out of control or that he was irrational. Jesus' action in the temple did not come from pride or ego. He responded to a condition that he found to be contrary to the purpose of the temple. The temple was to be a holy place of prayer, nothing less.

NOT TOO LONG AGO, I pulled my car into oncoming traffic not realizing how fast the traffic was moving. Glancing at my rear view mirror, I became aware that I had made the driver behind me very angry. He passed me quickly. About a block later, a truck stopped in front of us to turn left. I decided to go around on the right. However, the angry driver in front of me made the same decision at the same moment; we both pulled out simultaneously and both slammed on our brakes. He jumped out of his car and started yelling at me, whereupon I recognized him and said "Hi" and called him by name. He was still so angry that there was no hope that we would end the moment amicably. That was definitely an emotional experience, not one of feeling.

No matter whose fault that situation was, I vowed right then never to do anything again that might cause that much anger in another, especially the driver of a car. I played that unpleasant tape over and over for days in my head. Anger not only creates a dangerous situation, but it sends out waves of negative energy that are harmful to the well-being of everyone in the vicinity, if not on the planet.

SOMETIMES I THINK of negative emotions in the same way I envision the "seven deadly sins," which you will remember are pride, avarice, lust, anger, gluttony, envy, and sloth. These negative emotions have, for centuries, been the rule of thumb by which to measure our well-being.

In *What's My Type?*[13] (a book about the enneagram) each emotion is seen as a need:

Pride is a need to be needed;
Avarice (greed) is a need to know;
Lust is a constant need for more;
Anger is a need to be perfect;
Gluttony is a need to avoid pain;
Envy is a need to be special;
Sloth is a need to avoid, altogether.

The authors of the book suggest that each of us holds just one of these compulsions in our personality as the underlying key to our dark side. This is not to say that we do not possess other negative qualities, but there will always be one compelling negative trait in our personality. When that "sin" is recognized, we can then deal with it, bringing us a little closer to holiness. In order to identify our pervasive negative trait, we need to read the book—or try to observe exactly what it is that aggravates us in another person.

The enneagram actually adds two "sins" that I did not include in my overview of the system because they are not found among the classical seven. These two compulsions, which were added later, are fear and deceit. If we study each of the seven carefully, we can see that fear and deceit fit into most of the already existing deadly sins, if not into all of them. Deceit is how the sin is kept secret (even from ourselves), while fear alone would suffice for all seven.

It has been suggested that fear is the common denominator of all sin. If we read again the need that is part of the compulsion, we will find fear in each one:

Pride holds the fear of not being needed;
Avarice holds the fear of not knowing;
Lust holds the fear of not having enough;
Anger holds the fear of making a mistake;
Gluttony holds the fear of pain;

Envy holds the fear of being ordinary;
Sloth holds the fear of becoming involved and having to
    take responsibility.

Knowing that the underlying negative emotion is fear, however, is not good enough. We must recognize and name the fear. We need to know, "Fear of what?" Until we know this, the thought or action is a secret weapon that is used against us.

OFTEN IN SCRIPTURE, when Jesus is delivering a person of an unclean spirit, he will call the spirit by name and tell it to come out. It appears that to name the demon places it under the power of the person who is praying. It is the same with our own demons. First we need discernment in order to discover the predominant negative emotion in our own personalities. Only when recognized and named can that negative personality trait be transformed. We should not be surprised when someone near to us can tell us very quickly what our underlying personality dysfunction might be. This brings to mind the story about the priest in the confessional who said to the woman, "No, no, my dear, not your husband's sins, yours."

But if we are not brave enough to ask those around us what they see as our outstanding character flaw, then we must discover it ourselves. In order to make this discovery, we will listen carefully to our feelings.

WILL THROUGH FEELINGS

WHEN WE FAIL TO EXPRESS our feelings, our receptive centers become clogged until they can no longer receive clearly, and finally they shut down all together. Not only are we insensitive to those around us, but we fail to hear the still small voice of God. We are no longer aware of what our true feelings are, since we have denied them for so long.

A friend told me about a period of time when she worked in a home for the blind. She said that she and the other volunteers were fascinated by how they could always tell the difference between those who were born blind, and those who had become blind later in life. She described a small park behind the home with benches where the blind would sit and visit in the afternoons. The interesting phenomenon that she observed was how those people who were born blind sat and held one another as they talked, while those who had become blind later sat a polite distance apart.

It appears that we have been taught to curb our natural instincts and feelings. We have deprived ourselves of warmth and love by building an invisible shield of protection around ourselves. Each of us has a comfort zone that allows others to come within a certain distance when we interact. For some, this distance is fairly close; for others, it may be as much as four feet, depending somewhat on our cultural background.

In my time in New York with the Dalai Lama, I felt some embarrassment at how close this holy man sat to me as we talked. Later, I told my husband that there were moments when I thought he might kiss me since our faces were so close. I made myself sit still and not back up, which would have been a personal affront, and also I wanted to enjoy and participate in this holy man's high love energy.

Had this experience been with almost anyone else, I would have thought them to be forward, or strange, and I would have distanced myself. The difference is that the Dalai Lama has a highly developed consciousness. He knows that in reality there is no separation between us. We are one. And he is not afraid to recognize our oneness. What a wonderful world it would be if we were not under the illusion of separation and were free to love one another with the affection that I saw in the eyes of the Dalai Lama.

We can begin to get in touch with our feelings by observing how close we stand or sit to others. Try moving a little closer and see how it feels. Notice that we have different comfort zones with different people, as they have with us. We ask ourselves, "Why do I need to keep more distance with this or that person?" Is it fear of rejection? Is it disdain? Is it self-protection? Or is it that I have projected my own character flaws onto that person and therefore can't enjoy their close company because I don't enjoy my own?

Everyone has something to teach us. It may sound cold and impersonal to think that everyone is here just for our own instruction. But that could be true, just as we are here for their personal instruction since life is a classroom.

Have you ever taken note of the people you draw to yourself? I have noticed that the people around me are either to instruct me, learn from me, entertain me, be entertained by me, chastise me, be chastised by me, love and support me, or receive my love and support. Everyone holds a piece to the puzzle. All are for our growth, and we for theirs.

Often, in the midst of an unpleasant situation, I imagine a loud voice directly over my head saying, slowly and deliberately,

"THIS IS A TEST,"

and then suddenly the situation takes on new light. I am no longer caught. I own the moment, it does not own me. I am not a victim. I am conscious.

In order to observe our feelings, we must stay awake. We can take notice of how we respond to certain jokes, to criticism, to flattery, to gain, and to loss. Life offers us daily opportunities to examine our feelings. Every encounter engenders feelings/emotions that are either negative, positive, fairly neutral, or apathetic. The theater or movies are helpful tools for getting in touch with our feelings, as the scenes can be uplifting, entertaining, violent, provocative, frightening, or boring. In all these cases, we are able to watch how we react or respond. We can feel the feeling. As we get in touch, we ask, "Why did I react so strongly to that scene?"

I remember seeing *Jaws* for the purpose of observing my reactions. However, instead of observing, I became totally absorbed in the film. I experienced the incredible fear that the shark was meant to engender. I failed the test as I was taken in by the illusion. Unfortunately, that movie has had some lasting effects on me. For a very long time after seeing it, when I went diving or snorkeling, I was like a whirling dervish scanning the ocean for the great white shark.

AS WE GRADUALLY DEVELOP the ability to control our thoughts and our emotions, we will begin to appreciate the connection between the mind and the will. As we read on, we will see the power of thought and the need to control it, since it is, in a very real sense, prayer.

WILL THROUGH THOUGHT (PRAYER)

WHEN OUR OLDEST DAUGHTER was leaving home at age twenty-two I asked her, "Kathy, do you pray?"

She replied, "Who else can you think to?" I was relieved. Thoughts are always with us. For the most part, the thoughts that assail us day and night are excited by the emotions. We dwell on the things we long for and the things we fear. We do not usually think of this mental/emotional activity as prayer to God, but it can be because, "Who else can you think to?"

I doubt if God says, "Oh, she just bowed her head, I'd better pay attention for that means she is talking to me." Instead, we must realize that since God is always present to us, everything that we think or speak, becomes a prayer.

The two determining factors that surround the success of these prayers are faith and persistence, which come from a strong use of the will. The word faith can be used to describe one's faith or doctrinal belief system. Or faith can be an attribute of belief as it was when Jesus said:

> . . . *if you have faith the size of a mustard seed, you will say to this mountain, "Move from here to there," and it will move; and nothing will be impossible for you.*
> —*Matthew 17:20*

Jesus was telling us that we do not need a lot of faith. For it is not the quantity but the quality of our faith that matters. It is in absolute knowing that we can move a mountain that the mountain will move. When Carl Jung was asked if he believed in God, he replied that he did not have to believe because he knew. It is in knowing that we can walk on water that we can walk on water. It is in knowing that we can have perfect health that the miracle will occur. In Mark 11:24 Jesus continues:

> So I tell you, whatever you ask for in prayer, believe that you have received it, and it will be yours.

We create what we believe in, through faith. We co-create with God, and just as the worlds were created by the Word of God, we too create with our thoughts and our words. For:

> . . . faith is the substance of things hoped for, the evidence of things not seen.
> —Hebrews 11:1 (KJV)

Our thoughts contain the substance of the future. What is visible "was made from things not visible" (Hebrews 11:3).

AFTER FAITH COMES PERSISTENCE, the next requisite for fulfillment or manifestation of our prayers. In Luke 11:5-8 a parable is given by Jesus about one who asks a neighbor for three loaves of bread and is rejected the first time. However, Jesus says:

> I tell you, even though he will not get up and give him anything because he is his friend, at least because of his persistence he will get up and give him whatever he needs.

Combine persistence with faith and we are assured of receiving our obsession—for better or for worse. Job cried out:

> Truly the thing that I fear comes upon me,
> and what I dread befalls me.
> —Job 3:25

Since we create the things we desire and the things we fear Paul enjoined us:

> Finally, beloved, whatever is true, what is honorable, whatever is just, whatever is pure, whatever is pleasing,

*whatever is commendable, if there is any execellence
and if there is anything worthy of praise, think about
these things.*
                              —*Phillipians 4:8-9*

Paul knew the power and the danger of thought/prayer.

ABOUT TWENTY YEARS AGO, at a Christian ecumenical retreat, one
of the speakers suggested that we might claim Psalm 37:4 for the
desire of our hearts, "Delight thyself also in the Lord and he shall
give thee the desires of thine heart" (KJV). Immediately I began
to pray for a trip to Israel. I thought a lot about the trip at that
time and even planned it in my mind. Many years passed and I
forgot about it. Then one morning, while reading my Bible in a
hotel room in Jerusalem, I heard that small voice whisper, "Psalm
37:4." I didn't remember what that verse was about, but I opened
my Bible to the passage and there it was, the verse that I had
counted on for so long. My prayer (desire) had been answered.
At first, I was elated and gave thanks; but as I sat there, I began
to reflect on all the things that could have been my heart's desire
instead of that trip. I thought about my family and friends who
needed that kind of direct and intense prayer. I thought of the
hungry and suffering in the world, of leaders in government, of
clergy, of my own spiritual need, and more.

     I don't regret the prayer that made the trip to Israel possi-
ble; but I did learn from that experience the potency of repeated, heartfelt desire. I realized that discrimination was also an
important factor in my prayer life and my thinking.

PRAYERS FOR THINGS of the world and for worldly success may not
always be in our best interest. Prayer has to be examined to
determine the motivation behind it, which decides its direction—toward the light, or toward the dark. Why are we asking
for something of the world? Is it something we really need? Is it
for the building of the Kingdom and for the greater good, or is
it for the building of the ego? Our motive will determine the

outcome. Unselfish desire will create reality, while selfish desire creates illusion, our teacher. We can gain the world and lose our souls. We can bring poor health or disaster upon ourselves, for we are what we think (Proverbs 23:7 KJV). We have learned in medicine, through the use of the placebo, that thought is more powerful than a drug.

PART OF THE COMMISSION to stay awake is to pay attention to how we think, since thoughts may manifest themselves, depending on our faith and our persistence. We are also reminded that "what goes 'round comes 'round."

> *Do not judge, so that you may not be judged. For with the judgment you make you will be judged, and the measure you give will be the measure you get.*
> *—Matthew 7:1–2*

In other words, everything we think and do will come back on us. This teaching is part of God's law that we reap what we sow.

> *Do not be deceived; God is not mocked, for you reap whatever you sow.*
> *—Galatians 6:7*

Those things that manifest out of fear or unwholesome yearnings are created out of darkness. These negative thoughts bring forth illusion that will pass away, while prayers of light and love give us those things that will endure. In 1 John 2:15-17 we read:

> *Do not love the world or the things in the world. The love of the Father is not in those who love the world; for all that is in the world—the desire of the flesh, the desire of the eyes, the pride in riches—comes not from the Father but from the world. And the world and its desire are passing away, but those who do the will of God live forever.*

These words sound harsh when we consider that all God created was "good." How can it be that nothing that the world affords comes from the Father?

John is not speaking of creation as it was created by God but creation as it has been re-created by us. We have taken nature and distorted the ingredients to meet the moment with no thought of the next moment or the next generation. We have exploded the atom for our own destruction we have contorted the gene; we have mutilated our bodies with lust and drugs. We have co-created with the prince of the world, Satan. When John talks about the "world with its seductions," he is speaking of the illusion that surrounds creation. Creation itself is good; it is the way we manipulate it that makes it corrupt.

Just as we have learned through science that the world is not a machine but an organism, science has also taught us that the mind is directly related to the activity and performance of all matter. In *The Turning Point*,[14] the physicist Fritjof Capra observes:

> In atomic physics the observed phenomena can be understood only as correlations between various processes of observation and measurement, and the end of this chain of processes lies always in the consciousness of the human observer. The crucial feature of quantum theory is that the observer is not only necessary to observe the properties of an atomic phenomenon, but is necessary even to bring about these properties. . . . The electron does not have objective properties independent of my mind. . . . We can never speak about nature without, at the same time, speaking about ourselves.[15]

Apparently the mind has a direct influence on everything that happens right down to the atomic level. We have often heard, "Be careful what you pray for, you might get it." King Midas desired to have everything he touched turn to gold. The desire of his heart was granted, but he found that he couldn't live with the gift. Often we ask for something that causes harm to ourselves or to others. I wonder if we really know how to pray, or even how to think. I wonder if we know what is truly for our ultimate good. Perhaps the only prayer is, "Thy will be done."

THE WORLD IS OUR testing ground and Satan is the archetypal adversary. Remember that even the principalities and powers (the domain of Satan) were created through Christ and for him (Colossians 1:16); they were created for our spiritual development. And if we have learned the lessons that come from our desires for the things of this world, perhaps now we are ready to pray solely to God, to listen solely to God, and to live moment to moment in God's perfect will. At last our thoughts will be God's thoughts as they come through our undefiled intuition.

WILL THROUGH INTUITION

INTUITION IS LISTENING with the heart. The messages that enter through the intuition float softly on quiet music, they come while digging in the garden, or when taking a long walk. God speaks in the shower, or when a warm wind is blowing against our faces, or waves are pounding on rocks. Without doing a formal meditation I often turn out the lights and let the moon stream in the windows, while I sit quietly and listen. My mind begins to wander, and suddenly I think something that I have never thought before, or a question is answered. I am listening, and God speaks.

Intuition often speaks through what we call our conscience. Conscience is supposed to tell us right from wrong, but are we really sure we know God's voice? And has the conscience not been confused with misinformation about morality?

Conscience begins to submerge from the moment we are born as we are taught ethics according to the morality of those around us. It is for this reason that we cannot judge another. Because of this limited and fragmented perspective that we have gained from the world, we can say with Peter Russell "that I too, given the same history and circumstance, could easily have made a similar mistake."[16] But behind this often damaged conscience, which is ever changing, there is an inner voice that utters only truth.

When Helen Keller was told by Anne Sullivan about God, she replied that she had always known God, but didn't know the name. Likewise, Margaret Mead talked about the primitive tribes she visited where, by some name, each of them knew God. There is, deep within, an undefiled connection to the One. As we purify the body, the emotions, and the mind, we will hear God's voice.

Historically, there is an evolution of consciousness toward morality—toward God, goodness. There was a time when it was considered sport to watch people being torn apart by lions in the Colosseum. Even though barbarous acts are still perpetrated today, most of us are not complacent about them and, with a few exceptions, they are not done for entertainment. Generally we are shocked and horrified by inhumane deeds of torture, terrorism, abuse, or any depravation of freedom.

In October of 1995 Pope John Paul II spoke before the U.N. General Assembly. In his message, he talked about a quest for freedom, saying that there is a universal moral law written on the human heart.

> Freedom is not simply the absence of tyranny or oppression. Nor is freedom a license to do whatever we like. Freedom has an inner logic which distinguishes it and ennobles it; . . . We have within us the capacities for wisdom and virtue.[17]

Jeremiah 31:31 talks about this inner wisdom, and a time when God's law will be written on our hearts. And Jesus says to the woman at the well:

> Woman, believe me, the hour is coming when you will worship the Father neither on this mountain nor in Jersualem. . . . the hour is coming, and is now here, when the true worshipers will worship the Father in spirit and truth, for the Father seeks such as these to worship him.
> —John 4:21-24

When we release our will to God, we unleash the guidance within. Then and only then do we know true freedom.

As LONG AS WE ARE ATTACHED to the things of the world and live by the code of the world, we will not be able to hear the voice within. Meister Eckhart reminds us that it is where we cease to cling to things, that God begins to be. When we let go and truly relinquish our lives to Christ, we will begin to receive that pure inner guidance. Elijah spoke of hearing God, not in the wind, not in the earthquake, not in the fire, but in the still small voice.[18] When we hear that inner voice, we will desire only the things that are real—the things that will endure.

As we step out onto the water, Christ's hand will be extended to grasp ours, but we must not look down. If we allow fear to enter, we will surely sink. The emotions have to be transmuted before we can walk on water. While water is a symbol of the emotions, walking on water is a metaphor for control over the emotions—the second initiation.

We can best develop the ability to hear that inner voice through meditation: listening prayer.

WILL THROUGH MEDITATION

> For one soul that exclaims, "Speak Lord, for Thy servant heareth," there are ten that say, "Hear Lord! for Thy servant speaketh," and there is no rest for these.[19]

How much of our prayer time is spent in talking to God? How much time is spent in listening? Even if we believe that God hears our prayers (and thoughts), few of us believe that God speaks to us in return, which is a sad misconception. We don't hear God because we are not listening. We are called to rest in the stillness and to wait on God, who is eager, not only to be heard, but to take up residence in us (John 14:23). Here again, meditation is difficult for us because we have repressed the intuition. And then too we can't sit still.

Years ago I offered a class in meditation at our church. About fifty people showed up, and we sat in a large circle. A neighbor of ours, who had suffered three heart attacks, arrived as we were about to begin. I was delighted that he was there because I knew how good the meditation would be for him. After a brief explanation of how to sit, relax, and to meditate, we closed our eyes and began. In less than ten minutes my neighbor jumped up and started out the door. Turning to me he huffed in an out of breath voice, "I'm sorry, but I just don't have time for this."

It seems that those of us who need meditation the most refuse to make the time or simply can't sit still. For many, the channels have atrophied, or we can't seem to remove ourselves from the noise of life. Often people say to me, "It is simply not my nature to sit and do nothing." Meditation, however, is not passive; we are actively aware as we stay centered in our being, while the pleasure of meditation is cumulative. The more we do it, the more we want to do it, and the better it gets.

A STORY IS TOLD about two monks who were walking along the bank of a river. Suddenly they came upon a lovely young woman who was waiting for someone to carry her through the water. The monks had taken the vow of chastity (in thought and in deed), but at the same time, they were dedicated to a life of service, which presented a terrible dilemma. While the young monk was struggling over the decision, the old monk walked over, picked up the young woman, and carried her across the river. A couple of miles along the road, the young monk blurted out, "How could you? How could you just pick her up like that? Do you not care what people might think?"

The old monk turned slowly and replied, "Are you still carrying her across the river? I set her down two miles back."

ETERNITY IS NOW, neither yesterday, nor tomorrow. It is our habit of living in the past and the future that continues to keep us isolated from the Kingdom. How many of us destroy the moment because we can neither set down yesterday's event, nor refrain from fretting over tomorrow's task? How hard it is to see the eternal in this moment. In the sixth chapter of Matthew, Jesus said:

Look at the birds of the air; they neither sow nor reap nor gather into barns, and yet your heavenly Father feeds them. Are you not of more value than they? And can any of you by worrying add a single hour to your span of life?

And then he concluded:

So do not worry about tomorrow, for tomorrow will bring worries of its own. Today's trouble is enough for today.

Why is it that we allow our worries to rule our lives? All day and all night our minds buffet us about like waves on the sea. Can we not, like Christ, still those waves? Continuing in the sixth chapter of Matthew, Jesus tells us the eye should be single—beyond duality and judgment. When the eye is single, our mind is still, and we are focused. It is learning to live at the center of our being that brings peace.

OUR EMOTIONAL STABILITY or instability is reflected in the way we pray. Probably ninety-eight percent of personal prayer is taken up in petition. How often, in the midst of adversity and tragedy, are we able to praise God and give thanks? Scripture says, "In every thing give thanks."[20] Instead of recognizing that "*all* things work together for good,"[21] we are anxious and fearful. We tend to be reactionary, while reason forsakes us. Meditation brings us back to the center: the ground of our being.

Meditation takes a deliberate act of the will, a desire to sit quietly with God, to be Mary rather than Martha (Luke 10:41). It is good to create a sanctuary somewhere in the home. We can sit in a chair or on the floor. Ideally, we could sit on the ground by a running stream, or on a rock ledge high in the mountains, or on the sand by an ocean where we can allow all those worrisome thoughts to flee one by one. We close our eyes, sit straight and breathe deeply as we gradually allow our breathing to become lighter and lighter. Relax the head, face, neck, shoulders, back, arms, hands, legs, and feet. Focus the closed eyes between the eyebrows, in the center of the forehead, that we might see with the eye single. Now we are ready to retreat into our interior chambers. Let the thoughts come and go, and watch them go. Bring the mind to one point. "Blest are the single-hearted, for they shall see God."[22] Use *Amen* or *OM*, (sounds in silence), or the Hebrew *Yeshua* (Jesus), or the Aramaic *Maranatha*, which is to say, "Come, Lord Jesus." We could repeat, "I AM Love and Light," or let the Lord give us a word or a sound. Draw the sounds out and let the music hum in our body. Repeat the word or phrase silently with each breath. We will notice those old anxious thoughts trying to invade, but we are not to be upset by them since they have come to be healed. And as they are being healed, we simply let the thought go, and then return to our mantra (word or phrase). At first this exercise will seem difficult, but as we continue twice a day, beginning with ten minutes and then expanding to fifteen or twenty minutes each time, we will begin to experience an inner peace that will then move into bliss.

Meditation is the beginning of living in the continual presence of God. After a few months of this practice there will be a knowing that we are never alone as we find ourselves continually praying.

I remember when I first read the commission in scripture to pray "without ceasing."[23] I was sure that it could not be taken literally. No one could keep their mind on God twenty-four hours a day! And then one night as I was getting into bed, I saw an earwig scuttle between the sheets. I jumped up and threw the bedclothes down. I removed every piece of linen and shook each one vigorously. Finally, not having found the earwig, I remade the bed and got in. I read, talked on the phone, and finally went to sleep. In all of this, I never took my mind off the earwig. I dreamed about the little creature with its pincers stretched out to annihilate me. When I awoke in the night, I thought of the creepy little creature; and first thing in the morning my thoughts flew to the earwig. My mind had not been so consumed with anything since I had fallen in love with my husband. My question was, "If I could be that obsessed with the earwig, then why couldn't I be obsessed with thoughts of God, with love for my Maker?"

The pilgrim in the old Russian work *The Way of the Pilgrim* and the seventeenth-century monk Brother Lawrence in *The Practice of the Presence of God* both give us magnificent lessons in continual prayer. The pilgrim prays continually what has come to be known as the Jesus Prayer or the Prayer of the Heart:

Lord Jesus Christ
Son of God
Have mercy on me a sinner.[24]

(When I pray this prayer, I delete the last words, a sinner, because I don't want to reinforce the negative). The pilgrim prayed the prayer as he breathed in and breathed out, until his heart took over and every beat repeated the prayer. His entire body was in rhythm with it—became it—as he became one with Christ. Likewise, Brother Lawrence wrote:

> I worshipped Him the oftenest that I could, keeping my mind in His holy presence, and recalling it as often as I found it wandered from Him. I found no small pain in this exercise, and yet I continued it, notwithstanding all the difficulties that occurred, without troubling or disquieting myself when my mind had wandered involuntarily. I made this my business as much all the day long as at the appointed times of prayer; for at all times, every hour, every minute, even in the height of my business, I drove away from my mind everything that was capable of interrupting my thought of God.[25]

To have this continual awareness and inner calm is, first, an act of the will; then it takes practice.

A few years ago at a Buddhist–Christian Conference in Boulder, Eido Roshi, a Zen master, talked about the difficulty he had in his early prayer life. He said that he had a tendency to fall asleep even though he drank pots of tea. So he began to practice meditation while sitting on the edge of a roof. He said he fell off only twice before he mastered the art.

WHEN A CLOCK STRIKES, we can stop and take notice of where our thoughts are and bring them back to God. We can renew the habit of talking to God before we go to bed. Review the day and ask forgiveness for the things we ought not to have done or the things we have failed to do. Give thanks and praise to God, asking for guidance in our dreams. Then we can expect to be taught as the prophets were before us. Wake with praise. Give God the day and watch how well it goes. Rededicate the day throughout the hours. The morning shower will be a baptism, each meal, blessed by God, a sacrament. The air we breathe out dispels darkness and worry, bringing death to the old self. The fresh air we breathe in is an invitation to the Spirit of God to fill us with new life. Those we meet give us the opportunity to help them find Christ within, as we greet them with love and make them feel lovable.

Wherever we are, if we begin to feel agitated or fragmented, then it is time to stop and move into that quiet place within. Often at a noisy party, I slip away and find an empty room. There I close the door and sit in my familiar meditation posture. Within seconds, an inner calm begins to flow over me. Once again, I enter the silence through the Word. Then when I return to the gathering, it is no longer a noisy party but a room filled with sons and daughters of God, an experience of the resurrected life.

IN AN EARLIER CHAPTER I talked about some of the physical and emotional pain that can accompany intense meditation. But we can also see that the pain is worth our effort and even our suffering as the old refuse begins to surface and then to be healed. Meditation is about relieving stress that can come from the past with its tenacious roots, or it can be today's stress with flimsy green shoots. When emotions run high, they cause disruption that ultimately lowers our resistance to disease and creates a deficit in our ability to make intelligent decisions. But even beyond these costly limitations, we lose our connection to our Mighty I AM Presence.

When we are in a state of constant prayer, we sustain within ourselves Life itself. In every action, we give praise and thanks, recognizing the divine in all that is. Everything we think, say, and do is for the greater glory of God. God takes no pleasure in one who grovels before the throne. Prayer operates best when we allow ourselves to be lifted into God's presence where the treasure house of sacred gifts resides. The psalmist instructs us to:

> Enter into his gates with thanksgiving, and into his courts
> with praise: be thankful unto him, and bless his name.
> —Psalm 100 (KJV)

There, before God, we will begin to experience love, health, and consolations: the abundant life.

WILL AS HEALING

As with Job, the externals will change when we change. I am convinced that we bring suffering upon ourselves because of fear and guilt; and worse still, we tend to believe we deserve what happens. Jesus recognized this predisposition when he accompanied healing with the words, "Your sins are forgiven." And the paralyzed man stood up and walked.[26] Or again, when he asked the man by the sheep pool of Bethesda, "Do you want to be healed?"[27] We are a people burdened with shame and feelings of unworthiness.

A few years ago a friend of mine was in the hospital recovering from intestinal surgery. After the operation a blockage had developed, and he was in great discomfort as he awaited further surgery. While I was visiting him, I offered to lay my hands on his abdomen and to pray for the blockage to be removed. He was quite agreeable to my doing that, but as I prayed, I didn't feel anything happening; there was no energy moving through my hands. So I asked him, "Do you expect God to heal you?" After thinking a moment, he replied that he didn't really expect God to heal him because he didn't deserve it. (This is one of the kindest men I have ever known.) So we talked about God's unconditional love and forgiving nature, and at last he decided that God probably did want to heal him. Again we prayed, and this time I could feel the healing energy moving out the tips of my fingers. Then we heard a gurgling sound as the blockage in the intestines moved on. We couldn't help laughing. God is so good.

The Almighty does not dwell in the midst of negativity. When we feel unworthy, filled with guilt, or too mundane for the likes of God, we can't expect miracles.

SINCE SICKNESS IS SO often embedded in the emotions, we will find it helpful to use the emotions/feelings as aids in the recovery process. If it is through the personal will (the emotional level) that we have allowed illness or injury to enter, it is through connecting our will to God's Will that we can be healed. The same path that led to the illness or emotional disturbance is also our way out.

Seldom do physical problems originate on the physical plane, for the seat of dis-ease is found, most often, in the emotions. Once we can discern the source of the dis-ease, and know God's will to heal, then we will know how to pray.

I remember our healing team of five being called to the east side of Denver to work with a young mother who had been diagnosed with multiple sclerosis. She had no husband, but she did have several small children. Her condition was so bad that her mother had taken charge of her household. We asked the disabled woman how she felt about her children. She freely admitted that they were more than she could handle, even when she had been well.

It seemed fairly obvious that the illness had accommodated her by giving her the help she needed. The illness was real— physical—even though it had apparently found its origin in the emotions. We prayed and counseled accordingly, and there appeared to be a notable improvement in her condition at that time. Then we talked to the family members who seemed to understand that she was excessively overburdened. They all agreed to work with her until she was able to cope. The idea was to help her through a difficult time and then gradually allow her to take more responsibility. The treatment was similar to the way we might work with someone who has had a nervous breakdown. Later we heard that her condition had improved significantly. Healing can be as simple as that. Family/community is all about helping us grow up and get through the tough times, while counseling the patient is a critical part of the healing process.

We can counsel in a powerful way if we have first prayed for discernment. Then we connect our will to the will of God and expect healing. As we all know, healing can be physical, mental, emotional, or spiritual, while death is often the greatest healing. But when physical healing is appropriate for the person, and for the building of the Kingdom, then we will be shown how to pray for the body to be healed. In any case, we still begin our prayer asking for the root of the problem to be revealed. For unless the underlying cause is healed, the ailment will return.

After helping the patient find the source of the problem, we talk about forgiveness and reconciliation. Next we visualize wellness. It is helpful to have some knowledge of the human anatomy when we are laying on hands in order to visualize perfection—as we were meant to be. Often I call upon my guardian angel and the angel of the one who is sick to support our prayers. The presence of angels makes a significant difference. But even angels (some call them guides) will not act without our asking. Angels, too, respect our free will. After asking for help, we simply allow God's healing light to pour through our hands into the affected area as we give thanks. This radiance that moves through our hands is amplified by a feeling of love for the one who is in need.

Those who wish to serve in the ministry of healing must strive daily for purity of heart in order to release impediments to the healing light. We must live lives of peace and harmony where anxiety never hinders the work. Above all, there can be no spiritual pride, since all goodness comes from God and we are but instruments.

It is important for the healer to eat properly, rest, exercise, meditate/pray, and have fun. A light heart is more receptive to the flow of healing energy. We mustn't allow ourselves to be over-burdened with this work, for stress will diminish the power and cause us to lose our joy, our connection to God.

God's desire is always for healing, but not always for physical healing, and that is why we use discernment. Often we hear someone who has been to Lourdes, or to a similar place of healing, say they were healed even though they are left with the infirmity. God's ways are not our ways. There are times when people are healed, but not cured. Our own desires may have the best intentions, but they might not serve the ultimate good. Only God has the perspective of eternity.

CONVERSION: AN ACT OF THE WILL

AN INVITATION

THE LORD GOD CORDIALLY INVITES YOU
TO TAKE UP YOUR CROSS AND FOLLOW
IN THE FOOTSTEPS OF THE
FIRST-BORN SON

R.S.V.P.

GOD BECKONS US to take that leap of faith—to entrust our lives to the Master within. But because we have been taught fear, we are afraid to accept this invitation. It is often in a moment of desperation that we cry, "Lord help, I can't do it alone." Then, and only then, do we begin to relinquish our will in favor of God's will.

About twelve years ago, when I was going through CPE (Clinical Pastoral Education) to become a hospital chaplain, there was an extremely interesting case on the third floor of the hospital. A young man whom I will call Jim was undergoing exploratory surgery. After more than seven hours, the surgeon came out to the waiting room where I was sitting with his parents. The news was not good; cancer had filled his body. The doctor said they had done all they could do and that chemo-therapy was the next step. After the surgeon left the room, I turned to his parents and expressed my sorrow over the poor prognosis. Then I assured them that their son would be in my prayers. The mother replied sharply, "We don't want any of that God crap in his room."

In the ensuing weeks and then months, chaplains stayed clear of Jim's room—except for me. But I never talked to Jim about God. I did, however, visit him often and was able to observe a very sad young man. While he was in the hospital, his girlfriend left him; his parents, whom I learned were divorced, fought with one another in the room, and the doctors were not able to give him much hope. Several surgeries plus treatment had finally removed the cancer, but the scar tissue in his (already shortened) intestines would not permit the passage of food. He had been fed almost exclusively through his veins since he had entered the hospital.

Then, after eight months, about eleven o'clock on a Thursday night, I heard a voice say, "Go tell Jim about me." I was on the first floor and I literally ran up the steps to his third floor room. The general consensus of the staff on the floor was that he was dying. The door to his room was partially open, permitting enough light to enter the room so that I could see him lying there with his eyes open. He had lost a great deal of weight and had no hair left on his head. I had never seen him smile.

As I entered the room, he looked up with large sunken eyes. I sat down next to his bed and said, "Jim, I don't care what your parents think, or what you might think, we are going to talk about God, because it is God who heals. God heals through doctors, through surgery, through medication, but above all, through love, and I don't see that you are getting much of that." Then I proceeded to tell him the story of Job and how he was healed when he released his will to God. He had never heard of Job.

After a while he looked up and asked, "How do I do it?"

"You just say, 'God, if you are real, if you hear me, help me.'"

He did not respond, not a word. I kissed his bald head and then left the room.

The following Monday morning, when I returned to the hospital, I went directly to his room. He was sitting up on the side of his bed with a grin on his face and a toupee on his head. As I walked in, he looked up from the tray of soft food and said, "I did it." I asked if he had told his parents. His reply was a short, "Nope."

The last I heard Jim was doing well. He left the hospital less than a week after our last visit but kept in touch with the nurses for quite some time. I often wonder the direction his life has taken since he called on God for help.

As THE OLD HYMN reminds us, "Softly and tenderly Jesus is calling." That quiet voice is our undefiled conscience. The sound in silence will lead us from faith to knowledge to wisdom. The Lord cannot take that step for us. Only we can say, "I come" or "Help."

SOMETIMES IT TAKES an accident, a loss, or a serious illness before we realize our personal impotence and turn to God. We have all heard of the foxhole conversion. Sometimes life has to get pretty grim before we are willing to make that life-changing decision.

I remember calling Alcoholics Anonymous for some advice on what I needed to know about an alcoholic friend who was coming to visit. When I described my friend to the case worker, I said that she was at the bottom of the ladder. I explained that her husband had taken custody of their child and that she was living at home with her parents. The staff member interrupted me to say that my friend was not at the bottom rung and that her parents might be keeping her from recovery. She went on to say that my friend had never been allowed to hit bottom, and for that reason she was probably not ready to recover.

That reaction of the alcoholic case worker reminded me of something I had read about Teilhard de Chardin, the French Jesuit.

Père Teilhard had shocked a group of reporters during a discussion of the Nuremberg trials when he suggested that man must have tried everything before he could become fully human (humane).

Teilhard was not saying that each of us could or should try everything, but that as humanity is evolving collectively toward God, it will try everything. I ask, "What could possibly be left that we haven't already tried?"

We cannot lead a person into conversion until that individual is ready. Conversion means change, something that is not easy for most of us. Someone like Billy Graham calls from the altar to thousands of people and has hundreds of responses. Many of those who go forward are acting solely from the emotional level, and the apparent conversion is often not lasting. But the souls that are ready—those listening with their hearts—only need an opportunity in order to relinquish their lives (their will) to God. Those who have never had this experience do not realize what an overwhelming impact those steps to the altar (or up the mountain side) can have.

MANY OF US, THOUGH we have answered God's call, still find ourselves miserable and unhappy. We ask, "Why, if I have given my life to Christ, am I not experiencing God's Kingdom?" Conversion (change) is not just a once-in-a-lifetime occurrence. As in baptism, we are called, daily, to turn to God. Even though we have given our lives to Christ, there is always more to give. If we are miserable, the answer could be that we have drawn to ourselves what we need for our growth. On the other hand, it could be that we are refusing to relinquish those things that keep us from God.

In the midst of any kind of discomfort or suffering, I always ask myself, "What is the lesson?" I ask that question even when I stub my toe or break a dish. If we look carefully, we will see the attitude reflected in the question. Is it an attitude of self-pity, "Why me?" Or is it an attitude of simply "Why?" The fact is that there would be no tests and very little progress if all the days were sunny and all the beds were soft.

When St. Teresa of Avila was dumped out of her carriage into a mud hole she was heard saying to God, "If this is how you treat your friends, no wonder you have so few of them!" Even the saints questioned their hard times. But it doesn't negate the teaching; for every crisis is an opportunity for transformation.

I have a friend who is always smiling when I am late for our bicycle ride. Each time I apologize, she sincerely thanks me for the opportunity to practice patience—again. Life is made up of little lessons, opportunities for change, if we allow them. Once we have learned the lesson, we can move on.

ON THIS LEVEL OF WILL, the water is sometimes soothing and sometimes a rushing river that bashes us against the rocks. There are times when we can dig our feet into the sandy bottom of the river and hold tightly, and there are times when the current carries us quickly toward the sea. Right on course, we are being prepared for the fire initiation, where the mind will continue to be transformed.

WISDOM

Dancing before God
Delighting in life
How precious thy name
Lord Jesus

Sing it unto me
Swirl it round me
Send it forth
In luxuriant light
Colors multifoliate
Roses, rainbows
Riverlets of dew drops
From mountains
Filling valleys

Come dance with me
In me, through me
Come love with me
Through me
That I might create a
Vibration of love,
That all might begin to
Dance with me
In me
Through me

3

The Level of Wisdom:
The Initiation of Tents or Tabernacles
(Ascent of the Holy Mountain)—
Baptism of Fire

At last the hero is ready to realize the transfiguration.

Six days later, Jesus took with him Peter and James and his brother John and led them up a high mountain, by themselves. And he was transfigured before them, and his face shone like the sun, and his clothes became dazzling white.

—*Matthew 17:1-2*

When Jesus was transfigured into a Being of Light on top of the mountain, Peter, James, and John wanted to erect three tents, one for Elijah, one for Moses, and one for Jesus. The tent metaphor demonstrates that the apostles recognized what happened on the mountain as the ancient Initiation of Tents or Tabernacles, the third initiation. In this initiation, one is filled with *Shekinah* glory, which is the Hebrew name for the light (feminine) of God that dwells with or within us. Jesus, however, admonished the apostles for wanting to build a shrine that would again cause people to seek God outside themselves. For the experience was not to be unique, not to become a temple where we could worship, not to be relegated to a time and place in history, but an experience for all of us for all time.

Baptism in water is a rite of purification, while baptism in fire, though it also contains the idea of purging, represents the spiritual life, or revitalization. The ancients believed this third initiation to be from the Mother Goddess and called it "the ascent of the holy mountain." The light that shone from the face of Jesus on the Mount of the Transfiguration was also seen in the face of Moses when he descended Mt. Sinai with the Ten Commandments. It is the light that accompanies the renewal of the mind as Spirit takes up residence in us.

In the twelfth chapter of Romans, Paul entreats us:

> *I appeal to you therefore, brothers and sisters, by the mercies of God, to present your bodies as a living sacrifice, holy and acceptable to God, which is your spiritual worship. Do not be conformed to this world, but be transformed by the renewing of your minds, so that you may discern what is the will of God—what is good and acceptable and perfect.*

This passage is a summons for us to leave the illusion of this world and to enter into the reality of God. When we take on the mind of Christ, we are given eyes that see beyond the illusion. On the Level of Wisdom, we merge with the deepest part of our psyche, the soul, which then gradually is transformed into Soul, then into pure Spirit. As we purify the mind, we ask, "Is it possible that even Sigmund Freud was an instrument of the divine purpose?" And then, "Does psychology, ideally, not somehow fit with the teaching of the cross as we die to an undeveloped ego?" And finally, "Can we begin to love ourselves as we break beyond the constraints of the abused or damaged child?"

IN HIS SEARCH FOR GOD, T. S. Eliot was one of the most interesting people I have discovered. Eliot began his spiritual path on the couch of a psychiatrist. By following the chronological sequence of his works, one can follow his life. Between *The Waste Land* and *The Four Quartets* (from despair to the sublime), Eliot wrote the *The Cocktail Party*. In that play, the author depicts two paths to God. One is psychological in nature, while the other can be seen as a more direct (spiritual) path to God.

In the play, Edward and Lavinia represent a more or less typical English couple. The curtain rises on a cocktail party. Edward is trying to host the party having just read a note from Lavinia stating that she has left him. Without Lavinia, Edward finds that he is utterly lost; he doesn't know who he is. His identity has been derived from the way he sees himself in relationship to his wife. Alone, he has no self. Suddenly she has disappeared, and he is disoriented and bewildered in spite of the fact that he is having an affair with Celia, who is a guest at the party.

As Celia observes Edward's crisis, she begins to be aware of the tragedy of the human condition. Seeing through the farce of what is often called relationship, Celia feels a sense of being alone and of sin, but at the same time she feels compassion toward those around her. This incident causes her to change the course of her life; Celia has a conversion experience. Under the guidance of one whom Eliot calls a guardian, she joins a religious order, leaves England, and goes to a primitive island where she is martyred.

Edward and Lavinia seek guidance from the same "guardian" that guided Celia. In their case, the guardian takes the form of a psychiatrist (Alec Guinness in the original cast). The two, under direction from the guardian, gradually find an honest relationship where they can be themselves, on a course toward wholeness—holiness. Eliot thus shows us two paths to God, the psychological and the spiritual. While it appears that Celia has chosen the higher path of sanctification, both paths have led to an elevated consciousness, which will ultimately lead them to God.

This play was probably an attempt, on the part of Eliot, to show, not the merit of psychological counseling, but the importance of a renewal of the mind and the way we think. Eliot's *The Wasteland*, an earlier work, was written in the midst of a nervous breakdown that sent him to Switzerland where, providentially, he was directed to Carl Jung. Under the care of Dr. Jung, Eliot began to get in touch with his inner self, which later led him to write the kind of mystical poetry and plays that have inspired so many.

As we read the lives of the saints, we see that each one was, is, struggling with those barriers that keep us from purity of heart. Created in the image and likeness of God, we know there is perfection under the many layers we wear. Jesus challenged us, "You must be made perfect as your heavenly father is perfect." To be perfect is to love unconditionally. That love is within us; it simply needs to be unwrapped. Paul says that only with the mind of Christ can we judge "what is good, pleasing, and perfect." We will be allowed to judge because we will see with eyes that see the perfection beyond all appearance. On this Level of Wisdom, we will come to a new understanding of the nature of (what we call) reality. We will move from what we believe the world to be, to what the world is.

WHEN GOD SAID, "Let there be light," creation unfolded out of the Creator's very being. In the first epistle of John we are assured that God is love and light. Therefore, all that God creates is the divine essence of God, love and light (energy). Meister Eckhart wrote that "Every single creature is full of God, is a book about God." God is beyond nature (transcendent), as well as in nature (immanent), which is why we are drawn to the things of the world. We could even venture to say that it is the underlying divinity in matter that gives the things of the world their seductive quality.

Yogananda, the late Hindu swami, wrote that all men seek bliss. They think they will find it in money, and they are disappointed. They look for it in fame or in sex, but again they are disappointed. The search goes on until, in great despair over what the world has to offer (those things we have corrupted), they turn to God. Only in God do they find true bliss. So we cannot judge others in their mundane pursuits, for they are actually seeking God without that awareness. We are all on a quest for the Creator who dwells within and beyond creation. One day all matter will be changed to reveal its essence, divine light, God.

In 1 Corinthians 15:51-52 Paul reveals a mystery:

> We will not all die, but we will all be changed, in a moment, in the twinkling of an eye, at the last trumpet. For the trumpet will sound, and the dead will be raised imperishable, and we will be changed.

Jesus was changed on the mount of transfiguration. He showed Peter, James, and John a glorified body, our potential.

ON OUR TRIP TO ISRAEL, my husband and I were having breakfast one morning in Safad, where we were staying in a lovely old hotel high in the hills above the Sea of Galilee. We began to discuss our experiences in the Holy Land with a couple that was seated across from us. The man jovially asked if we had walked on water the day before when we had been down by the sea. We replied that we had not and we all laughed. But then he said, somewhat cynically, "You could have if you had known where the rocks were. That is how Jesus walked out on the water." I asked him if he was serious and, yes, he was quite serious. The good time was over and I too became serious. Since we had finished eating I stood up, walked over to his table, and then I told him that Jesus had walked on the water because he knew who he was. In full oneness with God he was able to raise the vibration of his body to the level of light, our innate inheritance. In this state he could walk on water. And, if we truly believed, we too could walk on water, for we are Beings of Light, Spirit. At this point my husband was becoming more than a little uneasy, so we wished the couple a good day, and left.

THERE ARE TIMES, when I am deep in meditation, that either someone knocks at the door or the phone rings. On some of these occasions, when my eyes open suddenly, I see myself and every object in the room as what appears to be vibrating molecules of gold light. The forms can be distinguished, but it is apparent that each object contains more space than mass. At these moments I am convinced my body could levitate, walk on water, or penetrate a wall. Then, as my awareness of the things around me becomes greater, the vibrational level seems to slow down, and I appear to be quite solid again. In that lower resonance I could eat with my companions, just as Jesus did after he passed through a wall in the upper room. There is no doubt in my mind that Jesus was able to move from a Being of Light to a being of matter (to raise and lower his vibrational level), at will.

There are stories about the apostles that suggest they understood their bodies as light. In the eighth chapter of the Acts of the Apostles, just after Philip had baptized the Ethiopian, we read:

> When they came up out of the water, the Spirit of the Lord snatched Philip away; the eunuch saw him no more, and went on his way rejoicing. But Philip found himself at Azotus, and as he was passing through the region he proclaimed the good news to all the towns until he came to Caesarea.

Philip's body had been teleported, from the road that goes between Jerusalem and Gaza, to the village of Azotus. Knowing God's respect for free will, we must assume that even though the act of teleportation or translation (de-materialization and re-materialization) was a gift of Spirit, Philip had some knowledge of what was happening. God does not use puppets. Philip, being in alignment with God, was able to use the gifts of Spirit at will.

In Einstein's equation $E=mc^2$ (energy = mass times the speed of light squared), the physicist tells us that energy and matter are equivalent. Jesus said, "I am the light of the world," but furthermore he said, "You are the light of the world" (Matthew 5:14). Spirit is our essence, our true state of being.

There are stories from East and West that will illustrate much of what we are talking about. Milarepa was a Hindu teacher who sat many years in the Himalayas eating only nettles. One day he said to his disciples, "Quick, get me tobacco."

They replied, "But Babaj, you don't smoke."

He answered them, "If I do not desire something I shall leave you." He was suggesting that he would ascend (transmute into light) without some reason for staying or some attachment to the physical plane.

Another story is told about the sixteenth-century Indian holy man Kabir, who had a large following of Hindus and Moslems. After his death, his devotees quarreled over who should be given his ashes. At this point the exasperated master sat up on his funeral pyre and gave his instructions. He said that half of his remains should be buried with Moslem rites and that the other half should be cremated with Hindu sacrament. Then he vanished, leaving a mound of sweet-smelling flowers that were disposed of as he had directed. Whether this actually happened is unimportant. The beauty is in the higher truth that is reflected in the story. We are beyond limitation. Even death has no hold on us.

In Genesis 5:24 we read, "Then Enoch walked with God, and he was no longer here for God took him." And in 2 Kings 2:11, Elijah and Elisha are walking along, conversing, when "a flaming chariot and flaming horses came between them, and Elijah went up to heaven in a whirlwind." Enoch and Elijah were assumed into heaven. They changed, in the twinkling of an eye, without the intermediary step we know as death. Tradition suggests that both Moses and Mary ascended, while Paul tells us that the last enemy to be overcome is death. More and more, we should be hearing of people who walk so closely with God that they are assumed into heaven without death to the physical body. The physical body will simply be changed, or returned to its true nature. One day, perhaps not so far off, all will be changed as we experience "a new heaven and a new earth."[1]

A NUMBER OF YEARS AGO, Bob and I were in Mexico City where we visited the shrine of Our Lady of Guadalupe. We saw the mantle that had been worn by Juan Diego when he was said to have had the miraculous visit from the Blessed Virgin. We saw how her image had been imprinted on the cloak. It was all there just as we had seen in pictures, but somehow I felt dissatisfied and didn't know why. Later our driver told us that in 1926 the church had hired an artist to enhance the image. Prior to that time, investigators could discover no pigment in the cloth. When the picture was retouched it apparently lost some of its luminosity. For over four hundred years the image has survived, but now it may fade, for only God's handiwork survives. In much the same way we have retouched nature, causing it to lose its luminosity.

Another curiosity is the one that surrounds the investigation into the Shroud of Turin. After Jesus was crucified, his body was wrapped in a burial cloth or shroud. The next day, when the women came to the tomb, the body was gone and only the cloth remained. This purported shroud was kept for years in Italy as a holy relic. After the invention of photography, nineteen hundred years later, an unsuspecting photographer snapped a picture of the shroud. The photographer found, to his amazement, that the negative revealed what could not be seen with the human eye—a clear image of what was believed to be Jesus himself. After many studies, a group of scientists in Colorado reported that the image was scorched onto the burial shroud with a photothermal flash of radiation. It appears that as Jesus passed through the shroud in his resurrection, his image was scorched onto the fabric.

Not only have these supernatural images of Jesus and Our Lady of Guadalupe appeared on cloth in strange and inexplicable ways, but the face of God is imprinted on all of creation. If we could see, we would see Christ (the light of God) in all the worldly kingdoms: mineral, plant, and animal.

IN HIS BIOGRAPHY on the life of St. Francis of Assisi, Theodore Maynard tells us that in his early life, Francis could not tolerate the sight of lepers, though they were not an uncommon sight in

Italy around the twelfth century. The author records these words that Francis heard in a small chapel one day:

> Francis, all those things that you have loved after the flesh, and have desired to have, you must now despise and hate, if you would do My will. Then the things that before seemed sweet and delightful shall become unbearable to you and bitter, and from those that you once loathed you shall drink sweetness and delight without measure.[2]

Shortly after hearing this, Francis was riding his horse back to Assisi when he came upon a leper in the open countryside. He told himself, "You are not a knight of Christ if you are unable to conquer yourself." He leapt from his horse and took the putrefying man into his arms and kissed him on the lips. After he had given him all the money from his belt, he got back on his horse to continue toward Assisi. On an impulse, he turned to look back. There was the dusty road and the open countryside, but no leper was in sight.

If we could only embrace what we find undesirable and, in so doing, see beyond the illusion to Christ! In Matthew 25, Jesus talks about feeding the hungry, giving drink to the thirsty, caring for the stranger, the naked, the sick, and the imprisoned. He said that when we do this, we do it unto him. He was speaking not only of baptized Christians but of the least of our brothers and sisters. Everyone of us is created in the image of God—from the divine light of God. And beyond this, those of us who desire it, are tabernacles of God's living Spirit. We will see and know this cosmic Christ when we are able to see through the many guises that each of us wears.

A few years ago I heard a priest say to his congregation that if he were to tell us that Jesus Christ was standing outside on the corner, he was sure that everyone would get up and rush outside. But he went on to say that every seat in the church was filled with Christ. It was true, yet we all sat there yawning, while he finished another sermon. No one heard the good news: Christ lives—in us.

IF OUR EXOTERIC (outer) religion does not lead us within to the esoteric (hidden, inner) religion, then it has failed. The purpose of ritual, liturgy, hymns, sermons, and prayer should be to inspire us and lift us up, for we are a deprived people without inspiration. The fact is that we are naturally evolving toward the spiritual, but there are steps we can take to facilitate the building of our interior light quotient, and the more we increase our own inner light, the sooner we can anticipate the establishment of God's new heaven and new earth, where the glory of God will illumine us.[3]

Fortunately, like bugs, we are attracted to the light and are moving away from the dark, which is the natural inevitable evolutionary process. In Revelation 21 we read:

> *I saw no temple in the city, for its temple is the Lord God*
> *the Almighty and the Lamb. And the city has no need of*
> *sun or moon to shine on it, for the glory of God is its light,*
> *and its lamp is the Lamb.*

John of the Cross called the transfiguration (Level of Wisdom) the level of illumination. For St. John, this was the middle stage that was preceded by purgation and followed by union with God. Teresa of Avila named this Level of Wisdom, the level of spiritual consolations. It is on this illuminative level that we receive the gifts of the Holy Spirit from which knowledge and understanding come.

WISDOM AS A BAPTISM OF THE HOLY SPIRIT

IN 1969 MY HUSBAND and I had been married eight years. The babies were out of diapers. Life was good. Janet (Bob's sister) and I had opened an antique shop in Evanston, Illinois that led us into many adventures. We had great fun attending country auctions and house sales in order to keep the shop supplied adequately with "junque." There were times when I would pack a picnic and pile all four children into a rented truck and head out for a day of gathering antiques. Then some Saturdays their grandparents would watch them while Janet and I worked in the shop. Bob and I attended church every Sunday and holy day. Everything seemed pretty much as it ought to be, but my spiritual life was at a standstill and I didn't even know it. And then one day a very strange thing happened.

We had been invited to show some of our better pieces of furniture and bric-à-brac at a nearby antique fair in Lake Forest. As we were wedging the last piece on the truck, I felt something akin to panic. We had forgotten the prie-dieu. It was a handsome piece of solid brass with a red velvet cushioned kneeler. I insisted that we take it. Janet couldn't understand my apparent anxiety, but we managed somehow to get the awkward piece onto the truck and to close the doors.

About mid-morning, the antique show was going well when I looked over to see a woman kneeling at our prie-dieu. Her husband was standing next to her, smiling. "Well," he said, "I guess you had better have that." And then he told her to write a check while he carried the kneeler out to their car. As she handed me the money, I surprised myself by saying, "You have something that I want."

"What is that?" she inquired.

"I don't know, but when I saw you kneeling there, I saw something in your face that gave me a feeling that I haven't felt since I was a young girl."

"Oh that!" she smiled. "Well, you shall certainly have it if that is what you want."

We exchanged addresses and phone numbers, then I put the incident out of my mind as Janet and I continued with the sale.

To my wonder, the woman called me early the next morning and asked me to have lunch with her that very day. I hung up the phone and started calling baby sitters. We did have lunch; and afterwards she invited me to her house to talk some more. She talked about something I had never heard of, a baptism of the Holy Spirit, a baptism of fire. She talked about people speaking (praying) in tongues and about a great outpouring of love. I asked a hundred questions and then left her house with a stack of books under my arm.

A few days later, I called her to ask more questions and she invited me to attend her prayer group. This was in the early days of the charismatic movement, and we had to drive about an hour north into Wisconsin to a Benedictine monastery in order to attend this almost clandestine gathering. That evening is not something that I shall forget. I had never seen people so happy, so open and loving. We sang, prayed, and yes, people did pray in tongues.[4] I felt like a released helium balloon as we walked out of the monastery long after midnight. When I got home, about two-thirty in the morning, my husband woke and looked at the clock. He couldn't believe that I had actually been praying with a group of monks until that hour. But that was how it was in the early days of the movement.

After a month or two of attending the prayer meetings, I felt that I was ready to receive the laying on of hands for the infilling of Spirit. But I was hesitant to go back to the Benedictines where I knew so many people. I feared that nothing would happen and that I would be embarrassed (heaven forbid). Something in me was saying that it wouldn't happen to me. I wasn't worthy. That was, of course, ridiculous. It is because we are not yet perfect that we need the power of the Spirit. We have only to ask. But because of my insecure feelings, I decided to drive about an hour or more south, to another monastery near Lemont, Illinois, where similar meetings were taking place with a group of Dominican monks. I went alone.

About halfway through the meeting, one of the monks asked if anyone would like to receive the Holy Spirit. I said that I would. The group gathered round me and began to pray as they rested their hands on my head. I felt nothing. Just as I had expected! One of the monks asked me how I felt, I just shrugged my shoulders. "Well, I'm sure you received the Holy Spirit when you were confirmed, perhaps that explains why you aren't feeling anything special," he rationalized. I was terribly disappointed as I left the chapel.

Walking to my car, I realized that a mid-winter ice storm was in progress. The windshield was thick with ice and the ground was treacherously slippery. At last I got the glass clear and the door un-stuck, but I felt great trepidation about driving home. I started to say a little prayer for a safe journey when, suddenly I was filled with an indescribable joy and began to sing in tongues. I sang all the way home without any fear whatsoever. My joy was reminiscent of that long-ago night as a child, in the Kentucky woods.

The exhilaration of that experience lasted for many months. During that time, I should have been locked in an upstairs room, for I was a typical "charismaniac." Although I was still praying and reading my Bible daily, the euphoria began to move into a more solid peace. I knew I had something to share, but I was convinced also that no one would listen to someone without any credentials, especially not to a convert. I decided that I needed to learn a lot more if I expected to be credible, so I signed up for graduate classes in religious studies. When I told the dean of admissions that I had no background in religion, other than Sunday school as a child, she smiled and exclaimed, "Great, then there is very little that you have to unlearn."

THE BAPTISM OF the Holy Spirit can be a gradual infilling, it can come during prayer, in a moment of compassion, or grief, during the sacrament of confirmation, or it can come when those who are already filled with the Spirit lay hands on us and pray for our infilling. I have never seen the Spirit fail to come to anyone who was open to receive it.

In that first year, I thought of the Holy Spirit as a gift giver. I had never thought of Spirit as cleansing fire, but that would come when I was ready. And it came. Gradually Spirit led me deeper into my darkness than I had ever dared to go.

Time elapsed and after years of enjoying various charismatic prayer groups, I felt the urge to move on. After the baptism, all I wanted to do was to pray, read scripture, and study. I am sure that the Spirit was behind my decision to go back to school. But it wasn't long before I was craving the silence that I was finding in contemplative prayer. Only later did I realize how my charismatic prayer experience enriched my meditation. Both charismatic prayer and contemplative prayer are important to a Spirit-filled life. From the baptism of the Holy Spirit come the gifts of the Holy Spirit:

> *To one is given through the Spirit the utterance of wisdom, and to another the utterance of knowledge according to the same Spirit, to another faith by the same Spirit, to another gifts of healing by the one Spirit, to another the working of miracles, to another prophecy, to another the discernment of spirits, to another various kinds of tongues, to another the interpretation of tongues.*[5]

But Paul goes on to tell us that the greatest gift is love.[6] We begin to see that goodness does not come from us, but through us, from the Spirit of God.

In contemplative prayer, we hear the voice of God and know the divine will of God. With the power and gifts of Spirit, we are now able to act.

WISDOM AS FIRE

Abba Lot paid a visit to Abba Joseph and said, "Father, I follow a simple rule as much as I can. I practice some fasting, prayer and meditation, and try to stay quiet. I keep my thoughts pure as much as I am able. What else should I do?"

The old man rose up from his seat, stretched out his hands toward heaven, and suddenly his fingers shone like ten flaming torches. And he replied, "If you desire it, my son, you can become all flame, even now."[7]

Jesus made it clear not only that he is the light of the world, but that we are also light. It appears, too, that we can become all flame, even now.

The Level of Wisdom, signified by a baptism of fire, holds naturally the element of fire. This initiation allows us to become transfigured beings, or Beings of Light. We rise above judgment into the understanding that all things are innately spirit and are moving toward Christ and the fulfillment of God's plan: the omega point.[8] There are no detours. The fire initiation is a burning away of the chaff; God's conflagration will consume the undeveloped ego.

In the fourth chapter of Matthew, John the Baptist says of Jesus:

> *He will baptize you with the Holy Spirit and fire. His winnowing fork is in his hand, and he will clear his threshing floor and will gather his wheat into the granary; but the chaff he will burn with unquenchable fire.*

Apparently it is chaff that God consumes. But what is this chaff? Is it not the husk that surrounds the seed? Is it not the mask, the persona, the defensive personality that the Lord will burn away? This passage from Matthew is not about the separation of the sheep from the goats. John the Baptist does not speak of those who are going to heaven and those who are going to hell. John is talking about the chaff or husk that surrounds each of us—the outer shell—that keeps us from being as little children. In 1 Corinthians 3:11-15 we read:

> *For no one can lay any foundation other than the one that has been laid; that foundation is Jesus Christ. Now if anyone builds on the foundation with gold, silver, precious stones, wood, hay, straw—the work of each builder will become visible, for the Day will disclose it, because it will be revealed with fire, and the fire will test what sort of work each has done. If what has been built on the foundation survives, the builder will receive a reward. If the work is burned up, the builder will suffer loss; the builder will be saved, but only as through fire.*

Paul tells us that we will be saved, but only as one fleeing through fire. The dross (illusion), which was co-created with Satan, will be burned. The foundation (Christ)—our essence—will be saved.

Then there is the final fire in Revelation 20:14-15:

Then Death and Hades were thrown into the lake of fire. This is the second death, the lake of fire; and anyone whose name was not found written in the book of life was thrown into the lake of fire.

We are told that those who have shared in the first resurrection[9] (the rapture), will not undergo this second death, this final purification, while those who have not yet been purged, must. I believe that the themes of holiness and fire are too numerous throughout the Bible to think that this purifying fire could be anything other than the consuming fire (love) of God.

I even believe that the purifying fire of God can be hell, but not for eternity. I often wonder how those who accept that heaven and earth will pass away,[10] and that death and the nether world will be hurled into the pool of fire, can expect hell to last forever? That is a total contradiction. So, what about eternal damnation?[11]

The fact is that the philosophical concept of eternity is not clearly expressed in either the Old nor the New Testaments.[12] Jewish thought has no idea of time, as we know it, and no concept of eternity. When the word eternity is used in the Bible, it is to denote an age or a period of time. Pure (mystical) Judaism is able to think beyond any concept of time and its limitations. Therefore, it appears to me that the passages referring to eternal damnation are only temporal. For ultimately, God will be all there is.

Referring to Christ, Paul tells us:

For he must reign until he has put all his enemies under his feet. The last enemy to be destroyed is death. . . . When all things are subjected to him, then the Son himself will also be subjected to the one who put all things in subjection under him, so that God may be all in all.
—1 Corinthians 15:25–28[13]

When God is all in all, we will have returned Home, where there is no duality between light and dark, good and evil. There will be only God. As I see it, in hell there will be payment for our sins for as long as it is needed. The fires of hell simply refer to the continuing purification that some will undergo. Since heaven and earth will pass away, or be transformed, we can rest assured that hell will also pass away, because "God . . . wants all men to be saved and come to know the truth."[14] And God, being God, will prevail.

When God is all, there will be no place for anything but God. If our work is unfinished on the earthly plane, it will continue in heaven. Catholics understand this continuing purification to take place in Purgatory, which may explain the many mansions, or levels spoken of in John 14:2.

Those who believe in reincarnation believe that earth is one of those mansions or levels where souls can return who still have earthly attachments, which would include addictions to food, alcohol, drugs, sex, money, or fame. These are attachments that can be gratified only in a physical body. Many believe that reincarnation explains suffering, especially among the young. Buddhists, who espouse reincarnation, also believe that some beings simply return to the earth plane to help those who are stuck here. These saviors of humanity are called Bodhisattvas. There is a beautiful story that illustrates the intention of the Bodhisattva.

> Three men were walking along a road when they came to a high wall. The first man climbed to the top and looked down into a magnificent garden. He was enthralled by the beauty of the garden and quickly leapt down where he was soon lost among the trees. The second man followed the first. Now the third man was equally taken by the odors and splendor of the garden; however, he resisted this eternal pleasure as he exclaimed, "I must return to find my friends so that I can bring them here."

Though we all want to enter the Garden, is it possible that we are here on the earth because we are not yet ready to enter? Or as Richard Bach says: "Here is a test to find whether your mission on earth is finished: If you're alive, it isn't."[15] Perhaps we will continue to return to earth until we get it right. We ask, "Have we been here before?" Does the purgation that we experience on earth and in the heavenly realms, then allow us to reach the perfection that the Master requires?

> *Be perfect, therefore, as your heavenly Father is perfect.*
> —*Matthew 5:48*

Paul says that we must work out our salvation with fear and trembling.[16] And if it is true that we resolve our attachments and our addictions on the earth plane and our spiritual shortcomings in the purgatorial realms (the lower levels of heaven), then where is the need for hell? Perhaps the suffering here on earth is part of our hell and our purgatory. In Genesis 19:24 we read:

> *Then the Lord rained on Sodom and Gomorrah sulfur and fire from the Lord out of heaven. . . .*

Again we see God fulfilling the role of adversary. We also read that the heavens are God's throne and the earth God's footstool.[17] In Psalm 139:7-8 we find God in the highest to the lowest realms of existence:

> *Where can I go from you spirit?*
> *Or where can I flee from your presence?*
> *If I ascend to heaven, you are there;*
> *if I make my bed in Sheol, you are there.*

We might suspect that heaven, purgatory, and hell are states of mind as well as places, for there is nowhere to go from God, not even hell.

WE ARE CALLED to that which is Real, that which will not pass away—the highest level of heaven. We can see this level of heaven in the closing vision of Dante's *Divine Comedy* where the entire universe is one perfect whole through the single flame of God's love and mercy. And again we find it in the writings of Teilhard de Chardin, a month before his death.

The joy and strength of my life will have lain in the realization that when the two ingredients—God and the world— were brought together they set up an endless mutual reaction, producing a sudden blaze of such intense brilliance that all the depths of the world were lit up for me.[18]

WISDOM THROUGH THE PURGATION OF THE SENSES

WITHOUT A SECTION on the purgation of the senses, a treatise on the mystical path would be incomplete. While many of the early mystics speak of purgation as a fiery cleansing, rarely do we hear them equate this cleansing with the gifts they receive. Often the gift is beyond the words needed to describe it. The fact is, however, that as each sensory organ is purified, we are handed a spiritual consolation. For behind every physical sense, there is an underlying spiritual sense, waiting to be awakened.

On our twenty-fifth wedding anniversary, Bob and I made a pilgrimage through Europe. Among the many sacred sites we visited was the town of Lisieux in the north of France where Saint Thérèse, the Little Flower, had lived. There, we saw the reliquary where many of Thérèse's lifetime possessions were displayed. As the two of us stood alone in the small room, we began to smell roses. Bob, with his scientific mind, observed, "They must pipe that smell in here."

When we left, I asked a nun if they had piped the smell of roses into the reliquary. She was a bit indignant as she replied, "*Absolument non!*" Then she asked if we had received the gift of the roses. We simply told her what had happened and she seemed so happy for us. Having considered Thérèse of Lisieux to be a bit of a wimp, I figured that it was her way of showing us how powerful and also how forgiving she is. But that was not the first time that I had received the gift of a special odor, just one of the many consolations.

THE RIGHTFUL PLACE of the senses is in the mental realm, since we can only experience the senses through some part of the brain. However, too often we allow the senses to tie us to the emotions, which then bind us to the earth plane. In the purification of the senses, we will work on breaking the connection between the senses and the emotions in order to lift the senses to the level of Spirit. In order to see, hear, taste, touch, and smell God, the physical senses must be purified through the refining fire of God.

Purification of the senses does not imply sackcloth and ashes. Seeing nature as good, we do not want to withdraw from it; in fact it is in embracing nature that we often discover the divine. Just as we withdraw from God when we fail to see Christ in our neighbor, we also alienate ourselves from God when we fail to see God in nature, the light within all of creation. Just as St. Francis talked to nature, we too can converse with God's kingdoms: the rocks, plants, and animals.

In working with the senses, we will gain knowledge of our own body and its sensations. This subject could easily be a book unto itself. However, I will only touch lightly on the five senses and suggest some exercises that will assist us in their transformation.

SOME PEOPLE ARE MORE sense-oriented than others. A few years ago I attended a lecture on herbs with a group of women. A large basket filled with herbs, dried flowers, and spices was passed about the room. Almost everyone became ecstatic over the various fragrances. I discovered something I have always suspected about myself: I couldn't have cared less. Fragrances are nice, but they don't send me into bliss. I didn't, however, admit this to the group for fear of being considered less a woman.

Though it might not be herbs, dried flowers, or spice that turn us on, at least one appeal to the senses will probably be able to lure us down the garden path. It can be the things on which we like to feast our eyes, sounds of erotic music, the aromas of the kitchen or the boudoir, the feel of silk, the touch of a soft breast, the taste of chocolate, or a vintage wine.

If our senses bind us to the things of the world, they do us no service. However, when we are able to see Christ in another, hear the "still small voice," smell a fragrance during meditation, taste the sweet drip of nectar from the awakening pineal gland, feel the Master's touch on our face or the soft breeze from Spirit, we are moving closer to true sense perception. Today these inner senses are being awakened with various therapies using light, color, sound, and aromas.

As we examine the senses, I am reminded of the Indian monkeys who would "hear no evil, see no evil, and speak no evil." I know that I have programmed into my mind lots of pictures and events I wish I had never heard, seen, or repeated.

While I am aware that much of the media today is true art, educational and even uplifting, I am also aware of the need for discrimination when watching and listening. Have you ever noticed how we tend to identify with a character from a book, a movie, or stage play? These heroes and heroines have more influence on us than we think. I have often said, "I am the book I am reading." Fictional characters and ideas have a way of grabbing us and then taking over our sense of self. Violent movies often feed a tendency toward violence, while scenes of lovemaking (tasteful or distasteful) raise the libido and excite the senses. In much the same way, advertising has the power to make us want to buy things we don't need. Magazines tempt us with all the superficiality that the world has to offer.

JUST AS OUR SENSES can lead us into folly, we are not surprised that those same senses can lift us into the holy of holies.

Gazing upon a flower, an evergreen, a blade of grass, or even a rock can open our inner awareness to the realization that God can be found within creation. When this type of meditation is practiced, the sense of sight is elevated toward God. In seeking the sacred in all that we see, we will recognize Christ in the AIDS patient, the woman next door, the derelict on the street, and in ourselves.

There is an exercise that I practice when walking or standing out of doors. I raise my eyes to the sky or to the horizon, which rests the eyes and at the same time refreshes the soul. Many years ago in Rome I was standing in the Borghese Gardens with a friend who had grown up in Rome. We were looking out over the lovely city when I peered down at a pile of trash that had blown up against the wall. I frowned as I pointed out the debris to my friend. Gently she placed her fingertips under my chin and lifted it up. "Look up," she whispered.

And the Psalmist said, "I will lift up mine eyes unto the hills, from whence cometh my help."[19]

Recently I visited the Monet exhibit in Chicago where I met an old friend for lunch in the Art Institute garden. She asked me if I had found the crowds to be a distraction. I was surprised at her question realizing that I hadn't even noticed that others had been present. I had felt totally alone as I moved from one room to another, observing the gradual evolution of Monet's style as he was able not only to see but to portray his awareness of the divine on canvas. Somehow light and the image were made one. And then in the last room, with the huge canvases of water lilies, I wept as I met the soul of the artist dancing among the lilies.

WHEN PURIFIED, THE SENSE of hearing can also elevate the consciousness. We know there is music that jangles our nerves, and there is music that soothes the soul. Sounds of traffic and construction can cause us to lose our tranquility, while a light breeze singing through the trees or the sound of the surf can lift our thoughts. But unfortunately, there are times when we seem to have little control over the noise around us.

When our four children were five years and under, before I had learned to meditate, there were times I would lock myself in the bathroom and run the water just long enough to regain my sanity. Tiny pounding fists on the door only enhanced the magnificent roar of an ocean that I had created in my bathtub.

Most of us have found that it is less a matter of what the circumstances are than of what our inner state might be. And it is for this reason that we set aside time for prayer and meditation. This time, well spent in meditation, changes the way we hear. The sounds of children become music . . . or at least a little less jarring than if we had not found the center of our being in the early morning.

The interesting thing about the mind and its distractions is that it works in series and not in parallel. There are certain automatic responses that we have built into the body, such as driving a car, running, walking, or for myself, knitting, that allow us to act in one way while thinking in other ways. However, we can only think of one thing at a time. If we believe that we can think in parallel, we will find, upon close examination, that we are simply switching back and forth at a rapid rate. Otherwise, there would be too much confusion for us if we were actually aware of everything going on around us at the same time. When I am in the dentist's chair, I practice focusing my mind elsewhere. It's hard, but I am able to ignore the noise and pain, unless it is really severe. Saying our mantra or the Jesus Prayer also works to help us shift our attention and then return to our center.

"Hear no evil" reminds me of a time when I was on the phone with a friend who asked, "What is that noise in the background?" I told him the kids were watching something on television. He suggested I put the phone down and go see what it was they were watching. I came back to report that it was a soap opera. He then said that I should be concerned, not so much for the teenagers, as for myself. He said they were watching television on the conscious level of the mind and that they were able to use the mind to filter out what they chose not to take seriously. On the other hand, while I was working around the house, I was listening to (hearing) the program with the unconscious mind, which meant that I was not able to edit what I was taking in. I had never thought before about how important it is to shield ourselves from unconscious distractions.

But I do know that we hear God in the silence. And for this reason, it is crucial to avail ourselves of silence. For there is a sound in silence that is the voice of God. There is the music of the spheres; and there is that divine whisper.

THE SENSES OF SMELL and taste really go hand in hand. But here I am reminded of a story that involves smell and sight that was told to me by a friend about Aldous Huxley. One day, when the two were taking a walk, they happened upon some fresh horse manure that was covered with flies. The English philosopher stopped to admire the shining, swarming obstacle in his path, as he exclaimed, "How extraordinary, how absolutely extraordinary."

As children, we are indoctrinated concerning what smells and tastes are pleasing, and which ones are disgusting. We were told, "Yum, yum" when something tasted good and "Yuck" when the taste was considered vile. We were taught to distinguish according to the preferences of those adults around us. My mother was an independent thinker who did not find the smell of a skunk's defense system unpleasant. And for that reason, I have never objected to that odor. So it goes.

As we grow up, we can develop new tastes and new ideas about what is pleasing and what is not. We can also learn to like (or tolerate) things that did not appeal to us as children. But I wonder, if we hadn't been programmed as children, if all smells wouldn't be "extraordinary."

A professor from the University of Colorado, whom I have known for many years, was going to India on a lecture tour and I asked him if he was planning to see Mother Teresa in Calcutta. He shuddered and said he couldn't possibly, because he wouldn't be able to stand the stench of the dying. I remarked, cynically, how fortunate he had been never to have married nor to have had children. How fortunate never to have changed a diaper nor to have cleaned up after a sick child. Or was that fortunate? The senses can be disciplined; they can be trained and they can be purged. Our senses need not have power over us.

TOUCHING AND FEELING are the final senses to be examined. There is only a small difference between touching and feeling, but for our purpose they teach much the same lesson. This area deals with the sensations that come through the body.

When, as a child, I would fall and hurt myself, Mother would ask me how that skinned knee was connected to my mouth. In other words, why was I carrying on so? This led me to be somewhat stoic about physical pain. However, it didn't help much with the lesser discomforts of life. My husband says about me, "Betsy is happiest when the temperature is between 68 and 72 degrees." And it is true, for I do like my warm baths and my pillow-top mattress. I used to take my down comforter when I went to summer camp in the mountains, but these days I am a little tougher.

When I read about the self-imposed hardships of Simone Weil, a Jewish ascetic who lived in Paris during World War II, I was deeply touched. Simone had a great compassion for her people who were suffering in concentration camps in Europe. For this reason, she chose to bear much adversity during the war. She fed herself sparingly and slept on the floor where the cold would penetrate her body. She explained that she couldn't live in comfort while others were suffering.

I felt shame that I had never allowed myself to participate in the physical suffering of the world in order to be one with it. So I started by turning down the thermostat. Not such a big deal. And then there was a period when, one day a week, I would eat only bread and drink water. This regime had been recommended by Our Lady of Medjugorje in Yugoslavia in some of her transmissions to the children. I know that none of this sounds like much of a sacrifice, but it was a beginning. Even when we refuse to answer a hunger pang with a between-meal snack, we are teaching the body who is boss. A fast is one of the best disciplines I know for training the senses.

When I spoke earlier of abstaining from certain foods and maintaining certain practices, it was more like going off and on a diet. But today, abstinence, meditation, and prayer have become a way of life. When I work in the area of self-denial, I begin to feel more in touch, not only with the suffering in the world, but with my own body. And then my prayer life improves, which reminds me again of the words of Thomas Merton: "Self-denial and sacrifice are absolutely essential to the life of prayer."

Self-denial is a means of knowing ourselves, our level of tolerance, our weaknesses, and the power of God in our lives.

THE IDEA OF THE PURGATION of the senses was taught by the Buddha long before the desert fathers in the Christian faith recognized the importance of renunciation. Buddha taught salvation from suffering. He said that all suffering comes through desires and attachments that must be overcome. In Hermann Hesse's book, *Siddhartha*, a book about the journey of a Buddha (enlightened one), Siddhartha realized that we must learn to "think, fast, and wait." In this discipline, Siddhartha found the peace of one who is no longer controlled by the senses.

As we observe the power the senses have over us, we are better able to find control. As a shift in consciousness takes place, we experience an inner power that was not previously ours. The desires of the world cease to own us. We are no longer lifted into highs that then drop us into lows. For when the pendulum swings high in one direction, it must then swing back almost as high in the opposite direction. This backswing creates our times of melancholy. These same highs and lows can be created by sugar, drugs, alcohol, and caffeine. As we abstain from these pacifiers, we purge the senses' desires which assists in our endeavor to rest at the center of our being.

If we are able to imagine a long pendulum with God at the top, we can picture ourselves at the bottom of the pendulum as it swings from one emotion to another. The higher we are carried in one direction, the higher we will swing in the opposite direction. But if we move up that pendulum, getting closer to God, the swing becomes shorter, until at last we move all the way to rest in God's embrace, where we will experience no motion (emotion) at all. Resting in God, we know that all is well. There we experience a joy that is permeated with peace and harmony—the Kingdom.

As we can see, the many levels of the Path are not necessarily taken in order, one at a time. They weave in and out; and within each level, we find the other four levels encouraging us to continue our climb. But we could not have begun to deal with the emotions until there was a semblance of order in our lives. And we would not have been invited to climb the Mount of Transfiguration until our emotions had begun to be transformed. We could not face Calvary without, first, having taken on the mind of Christ. And we would not, now, say yes to the crucifixion if we had not been enticed by the consolations of the spiritual life, to see, hear, smell, taste, touch, and feel Christ.

THE CROSS

Son:

To die alone I cannot bear
For it is cold and lonely there
Why is it you've forsaken me
To hang so heavy on this tree?

Father:

Never would you have left the cave
On this journey to the grave
If all of this you had known
For dying is to die alone.

4

The Level of Justice:
The Night Sea Journey—
The Crucifixion

There is a story about an aging movie star who went to a well-known photographer for a portrait. Before the photographer began, she leaned forward and warned, "You had better do me justice."

Without even looking up, the photographer replied, "What you want is mercy, not justice."

WE ALL PREFER MERCY, but what we seem to get is justice. Justice is God's law of retribution that is active whether we obey or disobey spiritual law. It is the left hand and the right hand of God. It is the law of cause and effect; we reap what we sow. However, beyond or above the law, there is already forgiveness, we only need to accept it. That was the message of Jesus when he said from the cross, "Forgive them; they do not know what they are doing."[1] In other words, "Poor things, they are ignorant of the law that they have put into action, they know not that what they have done will come back on them. They know not that they are killing innocence itself. They know not that they could cease to condemn and live eternally in a state of grace." God holds no grudges. It is we who have chosen to live under the law. When we fail to forgive or accept forgiveness we have condemned ourselves: a decision for spiritual death. Ironically, the decision for death on the cross—death to the ego—is a decision for life.

THIS FOURTH INITIATION is the culmination of the first three initiations: Order, Will, and Wisdom. On this level, justice is fulfilled, all debts are paid (canceled). On this level, we die the final death to the lower nature. And it is on this level that our lives are returned to balance.

There was a time when I struggled over the question of how another could take my sins and make retribution for them. How could one man take on the sins of the whole world? Was it a one-time act in all of eternity, or is it ongoing? These questions confused me until it seemed that I could either accept the teaching on blind faith, or I could deny it all together. But neither alternative would have been true to my nature, which holds a deep need to know and to understand.

And then one day I read a story from India about Neem Karolie Baba. Maharaji, as he was called by his disciples, would sometimes sit in the hot sun for hours or even days, wrapped in a blanket, sweating with a fever. His purpose was to pay some of the karmic debt of his disciples—to atone for their sins. In Matthew 5:26 Jesus warned, "You will not be released until you have paid the last penny." Hinduism teaches that every single debt must be paid in full in order to have a return to balance. The old Hindu guru, recognizing that the sins of his disciples were too great for them to carry, took them on himself. He was prepared to bear the burdens of his disciples, just as we are instructed to bear the burdens of one another.[2] Only when we realize that we are *one* can we see how this might be possible.

When I put this microcosmic example of the Indian teacher onto a cosmic level of the transgressions of all mankind, I began to grasp the incredible sacrifice that Jesus, as the Christ, made to save the world, his mystical body. When he said, "Father, forgive them . . .," he assured not only those at the foot of the cross, but all of us, that we are forgiven. The crucifixion broke the endless chain of retribution as we moved from the law to grace.

Though salvation was established in the realm of the highest heaven through the redemptive act of Jesus, we here on earth must still participate in the redemptive work that is unfinished on the earth plane. In Colossians 1:24, Paul professes:

> *I am now rejoicing in my sufferings for your sake, and in my flesh I am completing what is lacking in Christ's afflictions for the sake of his body, that is, the church.*

Theodore Dobson, in his book *Inner Healing: God's Great Assurance*, shows remarkable insight into the miracle of forgiveness and our role in it:

> When we forgive or are forgiven, something wondrous happens; things and people become real again. . . . For sin is a mask of unreality—it is a creature not from God but from man and as such it will not live into eternity. Sin is the "self" that we create to hide the real self that God has made. . . . When we accept or give forgiveness, we are cooperating with Jesus on the cross, making the world "real" again.[3]

After we understand Dobson's insight into the nature of reality, we must then wrestle with the implication that there is an unfinished aspect to the cross. He speaks of our cooperating with Jesus on the cross (just as Paul does) to make the world Real again.

Jesus did not die on the cross because of God's need for sacrifice, but for our need. God does not require human sacrifice. Jesus saved us through his love and forgiveness, not through death. But according to the old law of sin and sacrifice, Jesus satisfied the need for justice (balance).

In the cosmic framework, atonement was finished, the battle was won. Again and again Jesus called us to perfection. We have not taken that commission seriously. But until we do, our work is not finished. We are to be made perfect, just as Jesus was made perfect.[4] It was for this reason that he called us to the Path:

> If any want to become my followers, let them deny them-
> selves and take up their cross and follow me. For those who
> want to save their life will lose it, and those who lose their
> life for my sake will find it.

This requirement to be perfect seems impossible until we realize that perfection is not found in trying to be something special, it is beyond trying. Perfection is simply allowing God to *be* in us. It is in letting go, which can only take place through the grace of God. When we do fully grasp this concept, that perfection is in us, we will approach this fourth initiation with great excitement when we realize that it is this final death to the ego that will reveal our divinity: perfection.

IN THE NIGHT SEA JOURNEY, Jesus died and descended into hell where he spent three days, just as Jonah spent three days in the belly of the whale. In Matthew 12:38 Jesus told his disciples that the only sign he would give them was the sign of the prophet Jonah. This is the language of the fourth initiation, which was understood by those who knew the teachings of the mystery schools.

In the fourth initiation we die to anything that is not of God, which allows union with God in the fifth initiation, Love. It is only on the Level of Love that we can say with Jesus, "The Father and I are one."[5] In the Gospel of John, Jesus speaks as the Christ when he says:

> I am the way, and the truth, and the life. No one comes to
> the Father except through me.
> —*John 14:6-7*

It is the Christ in each of us that is our Way to God.

The Buddha tells a story about one who built a raft to cross a river. When he reached the other side he constructed an altar out of the raft that had gotten him across the river and there he worshiped the raft.

If we believe that the way is "out there" we have defeated everything that Jesus came to teach. I believe that this false understanding caused Jesus to say to his disciples:

> . . . it is to your advantage that I go away, for if I do not go away, the Advocate will not come to you; but if I go, I will send him to you.
>
> —John 16:7

Jesus realized that as long as he lingered on the earth we would look to him and fail to recognize that his Advocate (Spirit) is within each of us. To worship the man Jesus without recognizing the Christ in ourselves is idolatry.

IN THE FINAL WEEK OF HIS LIFE, Jesus completed the first three initiations in preparation for the fourth: the crucifixion. By the time each of us reaches this fourth level, much of our work has also been done, just as it was for Jesus.

When Jesus made his triumphal entry into Jerusalem, he already knew who he was and what his mission was to be; he had resolved most of the Levels of Order, Will, and Wisdom. The cleansing of the temple, the agony in the garden, the crucifixion, death, burial and resurrection would complete his mission.

The Level of Order began to be satisfied as Jesus cleansed the temple, bringing order into God's house. This concept is especially clear when we recognize the temple as a symbol of the physical body that is being cleansed to become a holy vessel for Spirit. Jesus completed the first as well as the fourth initiation when he died on the cross, which represents death to the lower nature. In this fourth initiation, Jesus' physical body would be returned to a cave like the one of his birth, where the Level of Order began.

In his descent into hell, which in some ways resembles the descents of Orpheus and Demeter, Jesus gave the sign of Jonah, three days in the belly of a whale. This descent was generally understood as the final death before the resurrection, where the seed would fall to the earth and die in order to bring new life.[6] In the same way, it was related by the ancients that the sun descends into darkness before it can rise again. Jesus was acting out, in a most extraordinary way, the path of the ancient hero as he descended three days into hell (or the lower levels of heaven) where he shared the Good News with discarnate souls.

Aside from the final work to be done by Jesus on the Level of Order, there was the Level of Will to be finished. What began with his baptism, and then continued in the wilderness with Satan, would be completed in this final week in Jerusalem. Jesus struggled with God over the release of his will to the point of sweating blood in the garden of Gethsemane. Finally he was able to give back to God that last bit of his will as he said, "O my Father, if this cup may not pass away from me, except I drink it, thy will be done."[7]

Next we move to the Level of Wisdom where Jesus shone forth his divinity on the Mount of Transfiguration. None of this was fully understood by his followers until he passed through his shroud—until he rose from the dead in his glorified body.

The Level of Justice was begun when Jesus denied Satan's offer of power in the desert and chose, instead, the cross. On the cross, he forgave the thief hanging next to him, and offered absolution for his mystical body (all of humanity) in the words, "Father forgive them; they do not know what they are doing." The fourth level was fully realized as Jesus uttered, with his last breath, "It is finished."

On this fourth level each of us will allow the cross to complete the work begun on the Levels of Order, Will, and Wisdom: the physical, emotional, and mental realms, as grace reaches out to bring us the rest of the way.[8] But in the mean time, we will continue to learn through God's law of retribution, a consequence of free will.

JUSTICE THROUGH GOD'S LAW

ONE SUMMER, A COLLEGE student from Japan stayed in our home for a short time. I had taken him on a picnic into the mountains and as we sat eating lunch, he began to express his feelings about the atom bombs that were dropped on Hiroshima and Nagasaki. I could only say how very sorry I was, and that we must all pray that nothing like that would ever happen again. However, with that encouragement, he continued to berate the United States. I was feeling some resentment as I responded, "Tomio, do you see the flower that is growing there?" as I picked a bloom. He looked at me quizzically. I proceeded to shake the head of the blossom over the ground and said, "You see that this one flower has many seeds, and next spring lots of flowers will grow here." He agreed. "Well, Tomio," I continued, "when Japanese planes dropped bombs on Pearl Harbor, seeds were sown. And in Hiroshima and Nagasaki, the fruit of those seeds was harvested. Just like the flower with many seeds, the harvest was great." ("When they sow the wind, they shall reap the whirlwind."[9]) We had a thoughtful moment; then I realized how self-righteous I sounded and lamented, "But it is true, the U.S. sowed seeds of destruction in Japan."

Thomas Jefferson said, "I tremble for my country when I consider that God is just."

The law of cause and effect will continue until we no longer perform acts of injustice. For this reason, Jesus gave only one law, which was to "love one another."[10] He understood that all the laws were under that one. The Bible speaks frequently of reaping and sowing, which was the tenet behind the practice of taking "an eye for an eye and a tooth for a tooth." However, God repudiated these personal acts of retribution, claiming, "Vengeance is mine."[11] It is not necessary to have personal satisfaction since God's law of retribution will always bring about justice.

Not long after the picnic on the mountain, I passed the window of a Christian Science Reading Room, which displayed a sign that read:

EVEN WHEN IT DOESN'T SEEM LIKE IT,
GOD IS GOVERNING AND YOU CAN TRUST
HIS LAW OF GOOD TO CORRECT AND
HEAL WHATEVER IS UNLIKE HIM.

We can trust that this universe, designed as our classroom, will always hand back to us that which is most perfectly earned; for it is God's justice.

Justice is reflected everywhere. When we make war and spit upon the earth with our pollution, filth, and waste, the earth reacts with violent acts of nature. When we lie, cheat, and abuse every law given by God, we will then reap what we have sown, for we are one with creation and with one another.

God's punishment is built into the system, for when we judge, we are judged.

> . . . give, and it will be given to you. A good measure, pressed down, shaken together, running over, will be put into your lap; for the measure you give will be the measure you get back.
>
> —Luke 6:38

When the pastor reads this passage on Sunday morning, we jump ahead knowing that it is a request for more money in the collection plate with a promise of abundance in return. But do we ever think of that same passage in connection with God's law? Do we ever stop to realize that an evil act will produce an abundance of evil, running over into the folds of our garments? Even though it seems at times that there is no punishment and that we are fooling a drowsy God, in God's own time there will be satisfaction, for it is the law, God's justice. The law is one of our best teachers, giving us the appropriate lessons that will eventually force us into, or prepare us to choose the God life. But there is a better way.

FORGIVENESS IS OUR way out. When we recognize our ignorance (our sin) and ask forgiveness, the law of retribution is broken. Punishment is no longer necessary when we ask forgiveness— and mean it. Forgiveness releases us from the law of cause and effect and returns balance. It was for this reason that John, recognizing the mystery of the cross, could say:

*God did not send the Son into the world to condemn the
world, but in order that the world might be saved
through him.*

—John 3:17

Jesus fulfilled God's law of retribution when he hung on the
cross for our sins. And he broke the force of the law when he
offered forgiveness. But if we do not forgive and accept forgiveness, the cross is meaningless in our lives. Whenever the
prophet of Hebrew scriptures warned of coming disaster, it was
always prefaced by, "Lest you repent." The law of retribution is
active, unless we repent, change.

It is important to remember that retribution is not only for
the one who sins but also for those of us who are unable to forgive the sinner.

I have found that the closer I come to the flame of God, the
faster the retribution returns for my edification. It is like a swing-
ing door that comes back to slam me in the face—instant karma!

On the other hand, forgiveness also works quickly. Sin, not
being of the nature of God and not being created by God, has
no ultimate reality, making it easy to erase. Since we create our
own darkness, we can also eliminate it. This state of negativity
has only the substance that we have given it, and will last only
as long as we hold onto it. When we invite in the light, the darkness will disappear.

AS WE HAVE COMPARED light and dark, we can compare life and
death. In Deuteronomy 30:19 we hear God say, "I have set
before you life and death, the blessing and the curse. Choose life
. . . ." We could say that God has set before us the real (life/light)
and the unreal (death/dark), the eternal and that which will pass
away. Only Love, the ultimate reality—the higher law—can
overcome.

In the Gospel of Luke we read about a woman bathing the
feet of Jesus with her tears. Jesus speaks to those standing
nearby:

Her sins, which are many, are forgiven; for she loved much. . . .

—Luke 7:47 (KJV)

It appears that our debt can be paid through the law of love, the highest law there is. Only the Christ could bring forth enough love to counteract the hate in the world; for there is no greater love than to "lay down one's life for one's friends."[12] Atonement was possible through Christ because the I am is the link within each of us to one another and to God.

Just as the Tree of Life is superimposed over the Tree of the Knowledge of Good and Evil, love is superimposed over the law of retribution. Life will come to us through knowledge and wisdom, while the law will shrink and die as it is supplanted by love.

The penitent thief, hanging next to Jesus on the cross, broke the force of the law of retribution when he recognized Christ, the fulfillment of that law, hanging next to him. The force of that law will be mitigated for us too, when we recognize Christ (forgiveness, love, and mercy) living in us. Love is above all of God's laws. Christ is the divine intermediary between God and man. The message of the cross is that *we are forgiven*. When we accept that message, Christ will not have died in vain.

JUSTICE THROUGH ST. FRANCIS

I RECOGNIZED THE fourth initiation when I made my profession into the secular Franciscan order. The fourth level demonstrates the final death of the ego. Though I am still far from initiation on this Level of Justice, the selfless life of St. Francis continues to teach me what I must do to allow this "death" into my own life. When we can look at the overall picture, and not get caught in our negative patterns, we realize that the process is really quite simple, which is not to say that it is easy.

I am reminded of a story from India where two men were standing under a huge tree that had thousands of leaves. The first man, a highly respected man of great wisdom, looked up into the heavens and implored God, "How many more lives must I suffer before I can leave this wheel of misery?"

A deep voice out of the sky replied, "Three." The wise man was greatly saddened.

"Three more lives, oh no. I cannot bear the pain."

Next, the younger man, known to be the town fool, looked up into heaven and asked God. "How many more lives do I have?"

The voice boomed, "Do you see the leaves on that tree?"

The fool replied with great expectation, "Yes?"

"That is the number of lives you have left."

"How wonderful!" responded the fool, "That many lives to love and serve you." With that, he was instantly caught up into heaven.

So there we have it. St. Francis acted the part of the fool, relinquishing all to God, loving and serving in all ways, while he ignored the pain or the cost.

But for most of us, the process is an ongoing one, until the day we can say with Christ, "It is finished." Release can come only when there are no more impediments between ourselves, God, and/or others.

JOINING THE SECULAR Franciscan order was not a step that I took lightly. My director worked closely with me for more than a year before I was sure it was a commitment that I was ready to make. I studied the life of St. Francis and aspired more and more to follow Christ in the way Francis had, which was with total abandon. I wanted, like him, to give up all for Christ. However, I was still a married woman with four children. How was I to balance my married life with a life of renunciation? Could I give up the things of this world? Gradually I began to realize that it is less a matter of what we have, in the way of earthly possessions, than how we understand what we have. Still, I had desires for things I did not need. Now I ask each time, "Do I need this, or do I only want it?" "What is the motive behind this desire?" "Is it to serve God, or is it to bolster my own ego?" I find that, just when I am no longer very interested in enhancing my wardrobe, or adding to the objects in the house, I can start to worry about aging. It is a never-ending battle. I try to remind myself that age helps us along the Path as it relinquishes, for us, the many desires of youth!

St. Francis took the vows of poverty, chastity, and obedience. I too wanted to take those vows. Weeks were spent in thinking, praying, and finally in writing them out. Poverty was to be a poverty of spirit, which meant that I was to be an empty vessel in order for Spirit to fill me. Poverty was also a recognition that all belonged to God and I was simply a steward of God's creation.

One day, during that time of thinking about the vow of poverty, I was driving through town when I saw a young woman hitchhiking who looked quite ill. I pulled the car over and she got in. I asked where she was going and she said that she wanted to go to the People's Clinic. I said I would take her there. On the way, she put some money on the dashboard. As I handed the money back to her, I said, "You don't understand. This is God's car, I just happen to be driving it today." She looked at me somewhat puzzled as I continued. "You are my sister, we are in God's car, and I'm taking you to the clinic." Just then we arrived at the clinic. She clutched her purse as she got out and slammed the door.

I heard her yell, "Crazy lady" as she ran toward the clinic. Of course, by the world's standards, she was right.

Richard Alpert (Ram Dass) once said, "The way I see it is that God grows wheat. Sometimes God grows it over here. So we call up North Africa and say, 'Hey, God's been growing your wheat over here, do you want to come get it, or should we just send it over?'" That's a world without fences—God's world.

If we practiced the kind of poverty where there is no me/mine, there would be no physical poverty left in the world. Someone once said that we would be amazed at what we could accomplish if we didn't care who got the credit.

Next was the vow of chastity. We are not talking about celibacy, but chastity. Chastity may be even harder than celibacy, but I am not qualified to make that judgment. It is true, however, that one can be celibate without being chaste. Chastity refers to a state of mind, or better, a state of heart. When a married person chooses chastity, it is a choice for monogamy in every sense of the word. In some instances this choice might include celibacy. I do know of cases where married couples have decided to live as brother and sister for the sake of the Kingdom.[13] But at this stage in my life, chastity means a monogamous relationship (in thought, word, and deed) with my husband, whom I love dearly.

Chastity in marriage sees physical union as an opportunity for two people to come together in cosmic union with the divine, recognizing Christ in one another. Two lovers with purity of heart unite to procreate and to come together to celebrate their love for one another and for God. They see God in the midst of their mutual love. When they join in union, God is present celebrating with them.

Chastity is a way of life—of thinking. The chaste heart denies hypocrisy and double-mindedness, while truth is practiced in everything. There is pain when we must admit to an indiscretion or a weakness, but when we realize the pain will come sooner or later, we opt for sooner in order to get on with the work. The questions become, "Do we only want to want God?" Or, "Do we really want God?"

And finally I took the vow of obedience. Francis gave his obedience to the church. I gave my obedience to Christ. The church should, at all times, be the manifestation of Christ. However, there are times when the church has to re-think its teachings, and at those times I know I am safe to have given my obedience to Christ, who will always lead the church into higher and higher consciousness.

My path, and the way I have walked it, is not to be normative for anyone else. We will each walk the Path in our own way. Though the levels will be much the same for all of us, the Path has many forks. For this reason each experience will be entirely different. Just as each level contains all the levels, the fourth level is present throughout our journey because on each level, in all we do, we are dying a little to our lower nature, and to our earthly desires. This "dying" comes through humility.

JUSTICE THROUGH HUMILITY

WHEN BERNARD OF CLAIRVAUX was asked what he considered the four cardinal virtues to be, he replied, "Humility, humility, humility, and humility." Thomas Merton understood St. Bernard well; he believed that humility can neither offend nor be offended.

Jesus spoke of humility when he said to his disciples, "I assure you . . . it is easier for a camel to pass through a needle's eye than for a rich man to enter the Kingdom of God."[14] The rich man represents our attachment to the things of the world and our refusal to let go of that illusion in order to follow Christ.

A friend told me that when he was in Israel, he was standing outside an ancient city wall where he observed a small opening that was referred to as "the eye of the needle." In ancient times, the main gates to the city were closed at night; but people on foot could pass through these small openings. As my friend stood scrutinizing the low doorway, he imagined how a camel might pass through. First the animal would have to be led by its master. Then the pack would be removed from the camel's back as it got down on its knees, lowering its head while its master encouraged it to continue through the small doorway. Only in this fashion could the camel move through the eye of the needle. Once it reached the inside of the city, it could stand tall again and the pack would be returned to its back.

We too must be humbled before we can enter the City of God. Humility of this type is not demeaning. Someone once said that "Humility is not thinking less of yourself, but thinking of yourself less." Scripture tells us that Moses was a meek man. He was a man with so little ego between himself and God that he could hear God, see God, and do God's will, as he yielded his own will. In the same way, Jesus was humble. In the fifth chapter of John, we read the words of Jesus:

*The Son can do nothing on his own, but only what he sees
the Father doing. . . .*

This kind of transparency comes from a death to the lower
nature that allows God to be revealed to us, and through us.

This transformation does not mean a loss of personality or
humor, or drive, as all of these qualities will be used for God's
glory; but it does mean that life will be seen in its proper perspective. God and the Kingdom will come first. All else will be
part of getting there. We will be stewards in this world of its
goods, animals, land, water, air, and sky as we reflect on the
words of Chief Seattle when he said, "The earth does not belong
to us. We belong to the earth."

IN THE SECOND chapter of Philippians, Paul speaks of the humility of Christ:

> *Who, though he was in the form of God,*
> *did not regard equality with God*
> *as something to be exploited,*
> *but emptied himself,*
> *taking the form of a slave,*
> *being born in human likeness.*
> *And being found in human form,*
> *he humbled himself*
> *and became obedient to the point of death—*
> *even death on a cross.*

When I read this, I am reminded of people who claim to be God.
Yes, we are created in the image and likeness of God, and even
of God's own divine essence. However, if something happens to
one of us, God will be just fine. But in defense of those who say
"I am God," I do have to admit that if something happened to
God (God forbid), we would cease to exist.

Until we have reached divine union with God, we are to
maintain a Savior/servant relationship with deepest respect,
love, humility, adoration, and even worship of the Most High. It

is through this attitude of humility that we can be filled. When we assume the role or title of God, we have limited God and made ourselves look ridiculous.

True humility is knowing the source of our strength and power. When we admit that all goodness comes from God, and that without God we are nothing, we have made ourselves available to be channels of divine love, wisdom, and power.

When Jesus said, "Come and follow me," it was not an invitation to a morning picnic by the sea; it was an invitation to commitment. A committed life is one that is willing to observe itself, and then be ready to relinquish its weaknesses to the consuming flame of God—even unto death.

Only with true humility can we surrender our weaknesses, our attachments, and our desires. We ask ourselves, "What am I willing to relinquish?" We look at our material possessions, our families, our home, our car, and our job. We test ourselves with the things of value that we own and imagine something happening to them, one by one, as with Job. What are our feelings with each loss? Can we then say, "The Lord giveth and the Lord taketh away; blessed be the name of the Lord"?

When we talk about possessions, it is better to look at the attitude behind the resource; for it is not so much what we have, as what we would be willing to release. Though our attachment to people seems so noble, they too must be released. When we lose our parents, our children, a spouse, a best friend, can we join Job in saying, "We accept good things from God, and should we not accept evil?"? In Matthew 10:35 we hear Jesus warn:

> For I have come to set a man against his father,
> and a daughter against her mother,
> and a daughter-in-law against her mother-in-law;
> and one's foes will be members of one's own household.
> Whoever loves father and mother more than me
> is not worthy of me; and whoever does not
> take up the cross and follow me is not worthy of me.

This is a severe instruction, and we would like to say that it couldn't possibly mean what it says. But the teaching is consistent with the teaching of the cross, and the sacrifice that is required, which is the sacrifice of our attachment to the world, and the things of the world. We find that when we bring ourselves to nought for the sake of Christ, then only Christ is left, above us and in us. Just as Abraham was ready to sacrifice Isaac, his firstborn son, to God, we too must be willing to sacrifice our possessions, our loved ones, ourselves. In fact, if we honestly have no problem with letting go of something, then we can probably keep it. Isaac was given back to Abraham only after the knife was raised.

Lastly, Job had to release his attachment to his reputation (self-image), and so must we. Like St. Francis, we may have to be fools for Christ. People can laugh, criticize, and say what they like, but if we allow unkind remarks to hurt us, it is because we still have "buttons" that they are able to push. (It helps to be able to laugh a little at ourselves).

When we can recognize and accept legitimate criticism, cease criticizing others, and let unfair criticism bounce off, we will have made a giant step on the Path.

Now we have arrived at the core of the teaching of the cross. Jesus commissioned us to deny the very self. He called us to unilateral disarmament. It would be easy to disarm if everyone else did the same, but we are called to disarm (to turn the other cheek) in the midst of ill-willed people. After all, what is it that we defend: the ego (our ideas), the physical body (which will pass away), our homes, when even the Son of Man had no place to lay his head? Our children? There are no children, there are souls who belong to God that have been lent to us. Do we defend life? There is no death.

I believe that most of us resist contradiction to the belief systems on which we have built our self-image and, therefore, we defend the ego. It is that insecure ego that must die, an ego that believes itself separate from God and from creation. We will find that when we let go, the difficult lessons will cease.

MANY YEARS AGO I attended a week-long workshop with Elizabeth Kubler-Ross in Colorado Springs. The workshop was limited to fifty people, about half of whom were terminally ill. The other half of us were people who worked with the sick and the dying. Dr. Ross had done much research in this area and, as a psychiatrist, had been able to help people work through the many stages of dying. She led us through mental exercises where we pictured, in detail, the loss of material things, then the loss of loved ones, and finally, our own illness and death. The final visualization proved to be easy after we had already let go of everything and everyone around us.

There is an exercise that goes beyond the one that I have just described. This activity comes from a Buddhist teaching and deals with the attachment we have to our own physical form. We begin by closing our eyes and with our creative imagination we watch the body begin to age and to deteriorate. Slowly the body succumbs to illness, and finally we observe its demise. After our death, we are aware of the decay of the flesh as it gradually putrefies and falls from the bone. At last we are nothing but our skeletal remains, carrion that has been licked clean. This may sound morose, but it allows us to have a rational attitude concerning our physical existence, which will continue to be temporal until death is overcome.[15]

Brother David Steindl-Rast once said, "Die when you are alive, because you don't know how well you will be able to do something that takes all your energy when you are senile, weak, or very sick."

When St. Francis let go of his worldly possessions and even his reputation, he was able to say, "Brother Sun, Sister Moon," since all the world was his. With a similar understanding, St. John of the Cross wrote:

Mine are the heavens and mine is the earth.
Mine are the nations, the just are mine, and mine the sinners.
The angels are mine, and the Mother of God,
and all things are mine; and God himself is mine and for me,
Because Christ is mine and all for me.[16]

To lose is to win, but the letting go is not easy. And just when we are on the brink of the final death, the darkness comes—the dark night of the soul.

JUSTICE THROUGH THE DARK NIGHT

IN THE SONG OF SONGS we read:

> *I opened to my beloved;*
> *but my beloved had withdrawn himself,*
> *and was gone:*
> *My soul failed when he spake:*
> *I sought him, but I could not find him;*
> *I called him, but he gave me no answer.*
> —Song of Solomon 5:6 (KJV)

This lament, from the wisdom literature of the Bible, surely describes what St. John of the Cross called "the dark night of the soul," which is the time when the Beloved (God) appears to have left us as we tread the Path. John of the Cross, a sixteenth-century Spanish monk and mystic, spent years in contemplation[17] and self-sacrifice before he realized union with God. This dark night marks the final stages of the Path when there is loneliness and devastation as we go deeper and deeper into ourselves, seeking the Beloved. But St. John found that divine union was worth far more than the price he paid in his years of mortification and devotion. A portion of the poem speaks of the ecstasy of the night.

> *Oh, night that guided me,*
> *Oh, night more lovely than the dawn,*
> *Oh, night that joined Beloved with lover,*
> *Lover transformed in the Beloved!*[18]

St. John found his Beloved in the void of uncertainty and solitude. From his experience, he came to believe that the dark night was a necessary part of the path into divine union with God.

Jesus endured anguish in the garden as he asked that his trial (cup) might be removed, and then his dark night on the cross when he felt forsaken by God. Jesus moved from a constant dialogue with God, to a place where he was alone. He walked through the "valley of the shadow of death."[19] When he cried out, "My God, my God, why have you forsaken me?"[20] no one appeared to be there; Jesus felt abandoned. It was a very dark night.

The dark night is the final and most difficult test, a time when many forsake the Path as the light grows dim. It is at this time that one might seek counsel, spiritual direction. Teresa of Avila once said that she would rather have a wise spiritual director than a holy one. And it is true that we need someone who knows and can explain the pitfalls and the consolations of the Path. We need someone who can recognize common spiritual phenomena such as visions, awakening of the psychic centers in the body, out-of-body experiences, bilocation, translation or teleportation of the body, locutions, certain sounds, tastes, and much more.

Even on the last levels of the Path, there remains debris from the first level. In the case of one suffering from aridity (a lesser form of the dark night), there is probably some area of that life that has not been healed. It could be an area that causes suffering from an unidentified guilt, some part of ourselves that has not been yielded to God, or an incident of abuse that we have repressed. Someone experienced in this kind of counseling would have little difficulty identifying the cause that might be hidden from the one who is in darkness.

God is not to blame for aridity, or even for the dark night, since God has no place to go. The dark night is caused by our own reluctance to release the world and to embrace the One. I was told by a monk who led a deeply contemplative life that in a few cases, the dark night is not necessary. Some find it easier to relinquish the things of the world than others. If we move toward union with God, with knowledge and understanding of what we must release, and do it, then it seems that the transition might take place almost unnoticed, except for that final moment of union when our beloved disappears.

As we read scripture, it appears that Jesus' first real trial was in the wilderness when he was tempted by Satan. For Jesus, this was a time of alienation from God as he pondered the possibility of earthly power. We all go through times when we are tempted by those things or experiences that might stand between ourselves and God's purpose for our lives. At that time, Jesus could have refused his mission; however, he chose suffering and death on the cross—union with God.

Most of the time, Jesus was aware of being in God's presence and felt a oneness with God. But then we hear him cry out to God, whom he believes has forsaken him. Why, in this most critical of times, would his Beloved have forsaken him? Perhaps this death was a decision that Jesus, alone, had to make. Theologians often say that it was at the moment when Jesus took on the sin of the world that he felt destitute, which could be the case. But I believe that his moment of feeling forsaken was the moment when he and his Beloved became one. There were no longer two; the dialogue ended.

In this final unitive state, there is a moment of intense grief as we no longer hear the one whom we have sought, found, and now seem to have lost. Where there had been two, there is now only one. "Lover (is) transformed in the Beloved."

When Jesus died on the cross, heaven and earth were rejoined. Jesus released his humanity in total acceptance of his mystical mission. Divine union was achieved and the Fall was healed on the cosmic level. The curtain between the outer court and the holy of holies was rent.[21] Jesus' purpose on earth was fulfilled. The deeply symbolic life had been led, showing each of us the Path to divine union. For Jesus, in his humanity, the dark night was momentary, because he had already died to all but this final duality between himself and God. Finally, when we are willing to relinquish even our relationship with God, union comes.

John of the Cross continues in the eighth stanza of *The Dark Night of the Soul*:

I remained, lost in oblivion;
My face I reclined on the Beloved.
All ceased and I abandoned myself,
Leaving my cares forgotten among the lilies.[22]

The idea of "self" is abandoned when we reach that place where we enter into bliss. All duality dissolves into the one.

This last step is taken by God. St. John calls it a "passive night," which is to say that there is no longer anything we can do. The Spanish saint had done the active work that only he could do. He had released all that he was humanly able to, just as the dying Jesus had done all that he could humanly do, when he hung on the cross. God would do the rest.

Dying is to die alone when all has been relinquished. If we have chosen the cross, we have opted to die to all attachments, concepts of boundaries, desires (even the desire for divine union). Now the moment arrives when we die—alone—the darkest of nights. But at the same moment we are consumed in absolute love and light.

BEYOND TIME AND SPACE

How limited we are
By what science
Calls space
But stranger still is
Time to us
With its penance
And its Grace

Someday we'll stand
Far beyond
The confines
Of this place

Where time becomes eternity
Space a vast infinity
And Love is master
Of all the human race

5

The Level of Love:
Born Again —
Resurrection/Ascension

At last we have reached the outer limits of inner space. And still there is more. Gradually we come to the realization that even the Level of Love holds within it all the other levels extending into infinity. But much has been accomplished. We have found order in the midst of chaos. We have consummated the marriage of Will and Spirit. We have stretched out our hands and seen our fingers as flaming torches. We have died the cleansing death of self. At last we are free to live as Spirit, as love. Now we can see God and hear God as we have moved toward holiness—wholeness, knowing that we are loved, that we are One.

Love is the only emotion that can transform. We can be told to love, but until love enters the heart, there is no real change. Love is divine and of God. All the water, all the sermons, all the liturgies in the world cannot do what love can do. Love begins on the very human level when parents accept and love a child. Then love is nourished as we affirm ourselves and others. For me, love burst into flame when I fell in love with the man I was to marry. During our courtship we began to change as our thoughts moved from self-centered thoughts to thoughts of the other. Then we were married, and in less than a year our first child was born, filling us with parental love that lifted us still higher.

When we love, the selfish ego begins to break down, and a portion of the will is relinquished to those we love, those we want to serve, which is the beginning of being able to love everyone and everything without discrimination. We are foolhardy to think we can love God without loving others, ourselves, and all of creation. Neither denomination, nor doctrine, nor dogma can save; love saves.

The Level of Love holds the element of air (Spirit), the Resurrection/Ascension, LOVE. This level holds the promise of the second coming when the Son of Man, Christ, the Messiah will come to us on the "clouds"—in the air.[1]

IT HAS BEEN ASKED what the world would be today if, instead of the cross, the symbol for Christianity had been the washbowl and towel that Jesus used to wash the feet of his apostles. The cross was Jesus' message at his first coming, but perhaps as each of us takes up the cross, we are preparing for the second message: the bowl and the towel. Recognizing Christ in all of humanity, we are now ready to minister to one another. We are ready to be of service to a world that has suffered hard and now longs to be healed.

Approximately every two thousand years the axis of our earth, astronomically, points to a new constellation in the heavens. These constellations were named by the ancients and given certain characteristics. Jesus' birth ushered in the age of Pisces, a water sign, that was symbolized by a fish. The Greek word for fish, *ichthys*, became an acronym for "Jesus Christ, Son of God, Savior." The fish was then identified with Jesus and the early Christian community. Much of Jesus' ministry had to do with this water sign. He was baptized in water, he turned water into wine, he walked on water, he washed the apostles' feet with water, while water and blood issued forth from his side at the time of his death. Water has been significant during most of the last two thousand years (the Age of

Pisces) as explorers have navigated the many rivers and oceans of our globe.

When Jesus directed his apostles to the upper room for the last supper he told them to look for "a man carrying a water jar,"[2] which was to foreshadow the washing of the feet of his apostles. But the man carrying the water jar is also the symbol of the age of Aquarius, an air sign, which I think of as Spirit. Aquarius is the age we are entering now as our earth's axis points to the constellation Aquarius. Perhaps this act of Jesus at the Last Supper also foreshadowed his second coming into the present age, which is to be an age of love and service where we are to wash the feet of one another.

An archetypal servant for this age could be Mother Teresa of Calcutta. We ask, "What can one person do?" and then we look at the little nun from Yugoslavia.

A few years ago a good friend of ours, who works with my husband, was on a business trip in India. As he stood in the airport in New Delhi, waiting for a plane to Calcutta, he realized he was standing next to Mother Teresa. Being almost six and a half feet tall, he bent down, introduced himself and asked if he might take her picture. She agreed as she smiled and smoothed out her dress. After the picture was taken, she turned to our friend and questioned directly, "John, what are you planning to do tonight in Calcutta?" Anticipating some kind of invitation, he hastened to assure her that his evening was free. She asked for a pencil and paper upon which she wrote out her address and then told him to give it to a taxi driver. He was to arrive by seven o'clock.

After an early dinner, John went promptly to the home where Mother Teresa lived with her sisters. He was ushered down a hall and into a room where the sisters were on their knees praying. John lowered his large frame to the floor where he spent the next hour or more in prayer. He said later that the good sister had tricked him, but he was not disappointed.

After evening prayers, Mother Teresa invited John and a few other guests to her cell where she served tea to the small group.

As they were leaving, John was the last to go out the door. Mother Teresa pulled on his sleeve and then placed her hand on his heart while she asked him if he had plans for lunch the next day. He knew it was another trick, but his heart was burning where her hand rested. He could only reply, "I'm free for lunch."

At noon the following day, with her instructions in hand, John took a taxi to what turned out to be the Sisters of Charity's home for the dying. When he entered what appeared to be a converted warehouse, he saw people lying on the floor on mats from one side of the large room to the other. A young nun approached him with a wash bowl and towel. An apron was wrapped around him as he washed his hands. Then he was led to a toothless old man who was lying on a mat. He was given a dish of porridge and was instructed to feed the dying man. John began to weep as he got down on the floor and gently lifted the man's head onto his lap. Then he fed him, spoonful by spoonful, with tears streaming down his face.

When John returned to Boulder, he called the office and said he wouldn't be in for a few days. He needed to rethink his life. To this day his heart still burns when he thinks of that life-changing experience with Mother Teresa.

WAS THERE A HIDDEN message in the man with the water jar and Jesus washing the feet of his apostles? Could Jesus have been pointing to this Aquarian Age for his second coming? Could he have been telling us that when we are able to grasp the message of the servant with the water pitcher—love and service—that it will be time for him to come again? It seems evident that human beings were not ready to serve one another, in love, two thousand years ago. In that period of time, there has been a huge evolution of consciousness taking place on the planet. Only now has the world begun to grasp the message of the cross (forgiveness and sacrifice) as many reach out to heal and to save. We each must ask ourselves, "Am I ready?"

Jesus said, "Stay awake. . . . You cannot know the day your Lord is coming." Are we awake or are we sleeping? Have we overcome selfishness? Are we leading lives of love, service, and sacrifice?

The Indian sage, Sri Satchidananda has said that everything we do, must be done for the sake of others. Our entire life must be a sacrifice. We are to think for the sake of others, act for others, live for others. Even eating, sleeping, drinking, and breathing should be aimed at bringing some good to others. He says, that if we live our lives in this manner, peace is guaranteed.

Every moment is a moment of crisis—opportunity. Jesus asked his sleeping disciples in the garden, "You could not stay awake with me for even an hour?" So it is with the world. We doze into delusion and believe that it is reality. For many, the curtain before the holy of holies was never rent, while most of the world is still stumbling around in the outer court. Caught in grief, in hilarity, in self-pity, in every type of emotion, we react to the stimuli of the world.

The pendulum of our emotions swings first in one direction and then in the other, higher and higher. But when we climb the pendulum and rest in God, we will know the peace that passes all understanding. With peace comes power: the power of God. With God we can heal the sick, feed the hungry, walk on water, and do "even greater things"[3] than Jesus did, because he poured out his Spirit on us.

St. Augustine tells us that miracles are not contrary to nature; they are only contrary to what we know about nature. As these miracles become more common, we will not be acting in an extraordinary way but in a very ordinary way. Like Peter, we cannot take our eyes off Christ, or we will begin to believe that the waves are real and fear will allow us to sink again into the illusion.

The mystic sees beyond that illusion into reality. As mystics, we see life as a testing ground, a furnace, not where iron is forged into steel, but where matter is returned to Light. We are aware, at all times, of our thoughts, emotions, words, motives, and actions. We are constantly praying. We are awake.

Awake, we will know our oneness and choose to do all we do for the sake of others. It should be easy now to see the limitations of another without judging, as we have discovered our own shortcomings and have ceased to project them onto those around us. Only now can we be of real service as we are able to see beyond appearance. Just in time, we are ready for the final trials that this age will bring.

As I SEE IT, there are two possible scenarios for our planet: transition through destruction, or transition through a shift in consciousness. Scripture prophesies both. But prophecy has always been contingent on repentance, as is seen in the story of Jonah. Jonah was a prophet who warned the people of Nineveh that unless they repented they would be destroyed. They did repent and were spared. We too must repent—change—if we are to be spared.

Scripture tells us that the trials and tribulations will be shortened for the sake of the chosen—for those who have heard God's call and have answered it. We must repent, not only for our own shortcomings, but for the sin of the world, for we are one.

It is time to recognize our sisters and brothers. It is time to cease all prejudice. It is time to feed the hungry, house the homeless, visit the sick, the aged, the lonely, the imprisoned, and the dying. It is time to educate our children, rid our streets of guns and drugs, help the single mothers and broken families. It is time to ask pardon for our neglect. And it is time to beg pardon of the earth itself for our ravages.

We have already begun to hear the sound of the trumpets[4] as the earth groans in the travail of birth. While we play out our final aggressions in war, nature lashes out to cleanse the earth. And the earth cries out to be swaddled in our love.

Love will not restore the old; love will build anew, as we move toward God. Not one step can be taken back. We are now ready to enter into the realm of Spirit as we end our delusion of separation, and allow God's divinity to manifest itself in us.

Violent destruction is not inevitable. Only we can make the difference; it is up to us. Even the idea of Armageddon is contingent on us. As we lift our hearts to God, we can release our old concept of what the second coming will bring. Heed the words of the Savior in Matthew 24:25-27:

> *Then if anyone says to you, "Look! Here is the Messiah!" or "There he is!"—do not believe it. . . . So, if they say to you, "Look! He is in the wilderness," do not go out. If they say, "Look! He is in the inner rooms," do not believe it. For as the lightning comes from the east and flashes as far as the west, so will be the coming of the Son of Man.*

With such stern warning about false prophets, perhaps we should re-think our expectations of the second coming of Christ. At this time the Buddhists look for the coming of another Buddha (the Lord Maitreya), Muslims await the Imam Mahdi, Hindus expect Kalki Avatar, or a reincarnation of Krishna, while Jews await the Messiah. But just as Jesus' first coming was not what was expected by the Jews, we might suspect that the second coming of Christ will be in a way that none of us anticipates, but in a way that answers *all* our prayers.

Perhaps he will come in a religion that is not Christian. Perhaps she will be Chinese or Nigerian. Perhaps it will come from another planet. Or, is it possible that Christ has done all that could be done in the flesh, and that this time, Christ will simply come in each of us?

"It is in them that I have been glorified" (John 17:10).

TOO LONG WE HAVE lived in separation from God and from one another. But we can all be changed in the twinkling of an eye. In each of us dwells Christ, waiting to be born—waiting to come again.

AND THE DAY CAME
WHEN THE RISK TO REMAIN
TIGHT IN A BUD
WAS MORE PAINFUL
THAN THE RISK IT TOOK
TO BLOSSOM.

—Author Unknown

Notes

Preface

1. See the quotation on page 7. The *Zohar* is a theosophical work, circa thirteenth century, that has been included in the Cabala (Jewish mystical writings).

2. Pierre Teilhard de Chardin, *The Hymn of the Universe* (New York: Harper & Row, Publishers, Inc. 1961), 32. This translation of the prayer, however, differs somewhat from the book.

Background/ Theology

1. The epigraph on page 23 is from *Fireball and the Lotus: Emerging Spirituality from Ancient Roots*, ed. Ron Miller and Jim Kenney (Santa Fe, N.M.: Bear and Company 1968), 28.

1. Mysticism

1. For information about Centering Prayer training and workshops, write: Fr. Thomas Keating, St. Benedict's Monastery, Snowmass, Colorado 81654 or call Pat Johnson 970-963-3964.

2. *The Climate of Monastic Prayer* (Kalamazoo, Michigan: Cistercian Publications, 1969), 56.

3. Matthew 16:24.

4. John 14:12.

2. The Path

1. St. Augustine, *Epistle* CII, ii, 12, 15.

2. Edward Carpenter, *Pagan and Christian Creeds: Their Origin and Meaning* (New York: Harcourt, Brace & Co., 1920), 24-27.

3. Raimundo Panikkar, *The Trinity and World Religions: Icon–Person–Mystery* (Madras: The Christian Literature Society, Inter-Religious Dialogue Series: No. 4, n.d.), 53.

4. Matthew 16:24.

5. 1 Corinthians 2:16.

3. The Fall

1. Genesis 49:9 and Revelation 5:5.

2. Plato, for one, believed that what happened on earth was a mere reflection of what occurred first in the higher realms.

3. John 12:31.

4. Frater Ackad, *Melchizedek Truth Principles*. Write to: P.O. Box 10771, Phoenix, Az. 80564.

5. Psalm 109:6 and Zechariah 3:1-2.

6. "Rulers and powers" are an extra group of spirits that may hinder the salvation of Christ. *Interpreter's Dictionary of the Bible K-Q*, 891, Ephesians 6:12, and Colossians 2:15.

7. Luke 22:31.

8. Adin Steinsaltz, *The Thirteen Petalled Rose: A Discourse on the Essence of Jewish Existence and Belief,* (New York: Basic Books, 1980), 30-31.

4. The Rise

1. A fundamentalist movement founded in the United States in 1965 with vague ties to Hinduism; it is not to be confused with actual Hindu sects devoted to Lord Krishna in India.

2. Revelation 6:1-8, 19:11-16.

3. 1 Corinthians 15:45.

4. Paul is reflecting here on Isaiah 25:8 and Hosea 13:14.

5. John 19:30.

6. Romans 14:11; Isaiah 45:23.

5. The Kingdom of Heaven

1. St. Bernard of Clairvaux, Canticle LXXIV, 1141 A.D.

2. A winged bull, or similar mythological beast, adopted by the Israelites from earlier Mesopotamian and Canaanite mythology.

3. "The Gospel According to Thomas" in *The Nag Hammadi Library* ed. James M. Robinson (New York: Harper & Row, 1977), 118.

4. Matthew 3:12.

5. Ephesians 1:4.

II. THE MYSTICAL PATH

1. The Level of Order

1. "Pastoral Constitution on the Church in the Modern World," Part One, Chapter One, The Make-Up of Man #14 in *The Documents of Vatican II*, ed. Walter M. Abbot, S.J. (New York: Guild Press, 1966), 212.

2. Simone Weil, *Waiting for God* (New York: Harper & Row, 1973), 134.

3. Sufism is the mystical branch of the Islamic faith.

4. John A. Williams, *Islam* (New York: George Braziller, Inc., 1961).

5. Proverbs 23:7 KJV.

6. Daniel 1:1-16.

7. Read *Diet For A New America* (Walpole, New Hampshire: Stillpoint Publishing, 1987) by John Robbins of the Baskin-Robbins family.

8. Genesis 9:3.

9. Grade B syrup is higher in nutritional value than grade A.

10. Quote found in H.P. Blavatsky, *The Secret Doctrine* (Pasadena, California: Theosophical University Press, 1963), 212.

11. Matthew 25:1-13.

12. The ones who have survived the great period of trial and have washed their robes in the blood of the Lamb (Revelation 7:14).

13. Fr. Anthony de Mello, *One Minute Wisdom* (Garden City, N. Y.: 1986), 11.

14. St. Teresa of Avila, *Interior Castle* (Garden City, N.Y.: Image Books, 1961), 53.

15. Matthew Fox, *Breakthrough: Meister Eckhart's Creation Spirituality in New Translation* (Garden City, N.Y.: Image Books, 1980).

16. Episcopal priest, Jungian psychologist, and son of Agnes Sanford.

17. The collective unconscious is what Jung explains as racially inherited psychic material (myths, concepts, ideas) that is present in every individual on the level of the unconscious mind.

18. Lucid dreaming is being aware that we are dreaming, and then being able to direct the activities of the dream.

19. In Luke 10:18 Jesus uses this imagery to recall Satan's fall from heaven: "I watched Satan fall from the sky like lightning."

20. God divided his oneness into two (masculine and feminine).

21. Romans 3:23.

22. Matthew 5:4.

23. Galatians 6:2

2. The Level of Will

1. Matthew 4:1.

2. *Interpreter's Dictionary of the Bible* A-D, 349.

3. Matthew 3:11 reads, "I baptize you with water for repentence, but one who is more powerful than I is coming after me. . . . He will baptize you with the Holy Spirit and fire."

4. 1 Corinthians 6:11, Ephesians 5:26, Titus 3:5, Hebrews 10:22.

5. Editor's note on "bathed" (John 13:10), *New American Bible* (New York: Catholic Book Publishing Co., 1970).

6. Monks who lived as hermits in the deserts of Egypt and founded the first Christian monasteries.

7. Revelation 3:16.

8. Matthew 25:14-30.

9. Georg Wilhelm Friedrich Hegel, 1770–1831, German.

10. Ceanne DeRohan, *Right Use of Will* (Albuquerque, N.M.: One World Publications, 1986), 1.

11. Matthew 21:12-14.

12. Luke 2:49.

13. Kathleen V. Hurley and Theodore B. Dobson, *What's My Type? Use the Enneagram System of Nine Personality Types to Discover Your Best Self* (San Francisco: Harper San Francisco, 1991).

14. Werner Heisenberg was first with this theory.

15. Fritjof Capra, *The Turning Point* (New York: Bantam Books, 1982), 86-87.

16. Peter Russell, *The White Hole in Time: Our Future Evolution and the Meaning of Now* (San Francisco: Harper San Francisco, 1992), 136.

17. Quoted in *Time*, October 16, 1995.

18. 1 Kings 19:11-12 (KJV).

19. *Letters of the Scattered Brotherhood*, ed. Mary Strong (New York: Harper & Row, 1948), 8.

20. Thessalonians 5:18 (KJV).

21. Romans 8:28 (KJV).

22. Matthew 5:8.

23. 1 Thessalonians 5:17.

24. *The Way of the Pilgrim* and *The Pilgrim Continues His Way.* Translated from Russian by R.M. French (New York: The Seabury Press, 1965).

25. Brother Lawrence, *The Practice of the Presence of God* (Grand Rapids, Michigan: Fleming H. Revell Company 1968), 33.

26. Matthew 9:2-5; Mark 2:5-9; Luke 5:20-23; and Psalm 38:4 on sin and sickness.

27. John 5:2-6.

3. The Level of Wisdom

1. Revelation 21:1.

2. Theodore Maynard, *Richest of the Poor: The Life of Saint Francis of Assisi* (Garden City, N.Y: Doubleday & Co., 1949), 45.

3. Revelation 21:23.

4. Acts 2:4,11; 10:46; 19:6; 1 Corinthians 12:10,28,30; 13:1,8; 14:5-39. A phenomenon where one speaks in an unknown language that is interpreted by someone else for the edification of the group. Read *They Speak with Other Tongues* by John L. Sherrill (Grand Rapids, Michigan: Fleming H. Revell, 1993).

5. 1 Corinthians 12:8-10.

6. 1 Corinthians 13:13.

7. Bro. Daniel F. Stramara, O.S.B., Dove Leaflet No. 21 (Pecos, N. M.: Dove Publications, n.d.).

8. Revelation 1:8,11, 21:6,13. Jesus is the Alpha and the Omega, the beginning and the end.

9. Revelation 20:5-6.

10. Matthew 24:35; Mark 13:31; Luke 21:33.

11. Though Christianity still teaches eternal damnation, there are many theologians today rethinking this doctrine.

12. John L. McKenzie, *Dictionary of the Bible* (New York: Bruce Publishing Company, 1965), 247.

13. Ephesians 1:10, 22-23 repeat this theme.

14. 1 Timothy 2:4.

15. Richard Bach, *Illusions: The Adventures of a Reluctant Messiah* (New York: Delacorte Press, 1977), 121.

16. Philippians 2:12 (KJV).

17. Isaiah 66:1; Matthew 5:35; and Acts 7:49.

18. Teilhard de Chardin, *The Divine Milieu* (New York: Harper & Row, 1960), 37.

19. Psalm 121:1 (KJV).

4. The Level of Justice

1. Luke 23:34.

2. Galatians 6:2

3. Theodore Dobson, *Inner Healing: God's Great Assurance* (Mahwah, N.J.: Paulist Press, n. d.), 184–5.

4. Hebrews 2:10.

5. John 10:30.

6. John 12:24-25.

7. Matthew 26:42 (KJV).

8. In the commentary of *Dark Night of the Soul* St. John of the Cross calls this the "passive night."

9. Hosea 8:7.

10. John 15:12.

11. Deuteronomy 32:35; Romans 12:19.

12. John 15:13.

13. Matthew 19:11-12.

14. Matthew 19:23-24.

15. 1 Corinthians 15:26.

16. *The Collected Works of Saint John of the Cross* (Washington, D.C.: ICS Publications, 1991), 87.

17. Meditation that transcends thought, which is the ideal in all meditation.

18. Saint John of the Cross, *Dark Night of the Soul*, English translation by E. Allison Peers of stanza number five from "En Una Noche Obscura" (New York: Image Books, 1959), 34.

19. Psalm 23 (KJV).

20. Matthew 27:46 and Psalm 22:2.

21. Matthew 27:51.

22. Saint John of the Cross, *Dark Night of the Soul*, 34.

5. The Level of Love

1. Matthew 24:30; Daniel 7:13.

2. John 22:10.

3. John 14:12.

4. Revelation 8.